"Dr. Boikai Twe is a master teacher who spent a life time building cultural leaders and stronger communities. His love and service to youths, community, and the African diaspora will be a source of inspiration to all who seek knowledge, truth, and beauty."
—Willis Bing Davis, founder and director of Shango: Center for the Study of African American Art and Culture

"The African Worldview of life is holistic and cyclical. When you meet Dr. Boikai Twe, you experience the continuity of the Pan-Africanism circle. He taught African American Psychology with such passion that community members and leaders lined up to take his class including myself. More than three decades later, the college still hosts the Pre-Kwanzaa Ceremony he initiated. As a transcontinental trailblazer, the Dayton community continues to solicit Dr. Twe's expertise and wisdom. *Grona Boy Go Zion* is a treasure for those who did not have the benefit of meeting him in person. The ancestors are smiling."
—Mama Nozipo Glenn, Dayton Africana Elders Council

"Not knowing your past is like embarking on a journey without knowing the destination. Through storytelling, Dr. Twe brings together heritage, literature, and psychology as instruments for nation-building. *Grona Boy* illustrates the wonderful ways God works to "lift the poor from the dirt and the needy from the garbage dump to seat them among princes." (Psalm 113:5-8) Reading this fascinating book will influence you for the better."
—Rev. Daniel A. Iselaiye, retired professor of philosophy

"A story strategically written. Clear, compelling, bitingly truthful, *Grona Boy* taps into the wisdom of our ancestors who teach the secrets of Earth and eternity. From the mind and behavior of a boy, his heart opens to receive unseen frequencies. Intellectual goals become a syllabus for divine guidance. Grasp how to live your knowing from a life lived as an instrument of collective consciousness; beyond the invisible field that connects us. Boikai is grouped among those special souls who master and magnify Zion on Earth. Asante sana for embracing us on your soul journey."
—BarbaraO, actor, filmmaker, and holistic health practitioner

Grona Boy Go Zion: A Roadmap to African Psychology

By
Boikai S. Twe, Ed.D.

Published by
Queen V Publishing
Englewood, OH
QueenVPublishing.com

Published by
Queen V Publishing
Englewood, OH
QueenVPublishing.com

Copyright © 2022 by Boikai S. Twe

The author guarantees all writings are original works and do not infringe upon the legal rights of any other person living or deceased. No part of this book can be reproduced in any form without written permission from the author.

Library of Congress Catalog Number: 2022902572

ISBN-13: 978-0-9962991-9-0

Edited by Valerie J. Lewis Coleman of Pen of the Writer PenOfTheWriter.com

Proofread by Sharahnne Gibbons of Something in Comma

Author photo by Shon Curtis

Printed in the United States of America

This book is dedicated to Elizabeth Flowers-Gibson and Charles J.L. Gibson, my mother and stepfather, who supported my education and professional development, and Mai Shaw Roberts, my grandmother, who inspired me to become a healer and a psychologist.

Acknowledgments

I want to thank Jack Bennett, retired professor of English, for reading the first draft of this project, offering suggestions for its direction, and writing the introduction.

Thanks to Lamarr E. Lewis, my former student and mentee, who wrote the foreword for *Grona Boy*.

Thanks to my Liberian team: Aaron Marshall, Martha Wea, Charles J.L. Gibson, Jr., Viola V. Johnson, and Aaron Mathis, for reading and providing feedback on the manuscript in Monrovia.

Thanks to my Dayton team: Kwaku Larry Crowe, Omope Carter-Daboiku, Furaha Henry-Jones, Bakari Lumumba, and Fayah Nyumah, who read and provided feedback on the manuscript.

Special thanks to my wife, Deborah D. Twe, and sons, Emman B. Twe, Dakona K. Twe, and Thomas A. Massaquoi for their support and inspiration.

Table of Contents

Foreword by Lamarr E. Lewis 9
Introduction by Professor Jack A. Bennett 11
Chapter 1: Going Zion 13
Chapter 2: Self-Knowledge 25
Chapter 3: Blackness - Melanin Magic 39
Chapter 4: Black Migration and Repatriation 47
Chapter 5: Lifecycle in a Village 55
Chapter 6: Parenthood 61
Chapter 7: Spirituality 65
Chapter 8: Disorientation and Disorders 77
Chapter 9: The Art and Science of Healing 83
Chapter 10: Community Psychology 89
Chapter 11: Rastafari Community 95
Chapter 12: Ujamaa: Cooperative Economics 101
Chapter 13: Africana Studies 107
Chapter 14: Dayton Rites of Passage and ABLE Youth Leadership Institute 111
Chapter 15: Black Lives Matter 117
Chapter 16: Economic Community of West Africa and African Union 123
Chapter 17: Building for Eternity 131
Chapter 18: Vulnerable and Empowered 137
Chapter 19: Making Music 143

Chapter 20: Libation to Ancestors 149
Chapter 21: Africa 2063 153
Chapter 22: Opening Zion's Gates 163
About the Author... 167
About Queen V Publishing 169

Foreword by Lamarr E. Lewis

I have heard it said that youth is wasted on the young. I agree with that sentiment because my youth is in the rearview mirror, but not too far. However, during those days of blissful ignorance, I met a man who changed my life. He provided guidance and direction when I needed it most. That man is Dr. Boikai Sellassie Twe.

Nineteen-years-old and at a pivotal stage in my development, I coped with childhood wounds, disappointments, and emerging adulthood. I wanted to make sense of the world and my place in it. In this quandary of colliding realities, Dr. Twe chose me to lead the African American Culture Club at Sinclair Community College. Seemingly a random choice, he may never know how much he changed my life.

Dr. Twe instilled in me effective leadership, critical thinking, and just as important, pride in myself and my culture. Through his mentorship, I was challenged to be a community leader, change agent, and role model for those coming after me. Armed with his sage advice, I embarked on my hero's journey and found my true passion…community-based mental health. I am an authority in this field and a healer of the most fragile among us. I KNOW I would not have done anything close to this profession without his influence and support.

To be gifted with not only the desire to help the next generation, but the knowledge and wisdom to do so, makes him an expert in youth engagement and leadership development. His expertise has changed the lives of countless others.

Grona Boy Go Zion gave me deeper understanding of the path he took to become the man I admire. His love for his people and culture is unparalleled. The depth of his wisdom knows no bounds and is recognized as a vanguard in the Black psychology movement. I hope you get as much from this book as I did. If you get a touch of what Dr. Twe has to offer, your life will change for the better.

> "A leader who does not take advice is not a leader."
> —Kenyan Proverb

Thank you for teaching me how to lead, Dr. Twe.

Peace and power to all who strive.

Lamarr E. Lewis, MA LAPC CPRP
LewisFamilyConsulting.net

Introduction by Professor Jack A. Bennett

"Let the nations of the world respect the integrity and independence of the free Negro states of Abyssinia, Liberia, Haiti and the rest, and let the inhabitants of these states, the independent tribes of Africa, the Negroes of the West Indies and America, and the Black subjects of all nations take courage, strive ceaselessly and, fight bravely, that they may prove to the world their incontestable right to be counted among the great brotherhood of mankind."
— W.E.B. Du Bois

Self-identification, self-determination, and global unification have been the passionate quest of the people along the African diaspora for centuries. It transcended from the philosophies, societal analytics, and revolutionary organizations of our elders into the modern activism of our youth, as it should be. The words of Du Bois and others provide the scholastic shoulders for a young Liberian to launch his quest toward understanding the academic world before him.

The process of self-discovery became the quintessential element of his being. The desire to connect his past demanded that he invoked the wisdom of his ancestors, embraced their thoughts and words, and spun them into lifelong virtues that will be guideposts that benefited him.

In *Grona Boy Go Zion*, we are privy to this process. With the mighty roar of the ocean as a backdrop, he explored the dynamic powers that nature, time, and circumstances held over the development of the plight of the world's people. Twe's work is not only a biographical portrait, but an introduction to Pan-Africanism and African American psychology.

At Sinclair Community College, Twe created a curriculum and programs that teach students and Miami Valley residents the embodiment of values for better living. He strives to show the ancestral link among Africans and African Americans that demands to be endeared if we are to survive and grow. He assures us that we all are that "Black Spark."

    Jack A. Bennett
    Professor Emeritus English
    Sinclair Community College

Chapter 1

Going Zion

A Pan-African life is the best way to describe my fifty years of study and practice in African psychology. The African Union flag, depicted as the sun on the front cover, is a signpost to Pan Africanism and a symbol of Zion. My journey took me many places, which led me from the darkness of self-doubt into the light of righteous living…Zion. This story describes my development as a psychologist and what I learned along the way.

My father, H. Carey Thomas, was born in Brewerville. His family settled there as Baptist missionaries from Barbados. This town was established in the 1870s by U.S. African American settlers, African immigrants and missionaries from the Caribbean, Africans rescued from slave ships on the Atlantic Ocean, and Gola and Vai people who lived in surrounding villages. Brewerville is located along the St. Paul River facing the Atlantic Ocean. We were called "up-river" people because we relied on the river for travel and trade.

My mother, Elizabeth Flowers, was also born in Brewerville, where her family settled from America. She and her siblings attended Lott Carey Mission School operated by my father's family. Going to school was a priority in Brewerville.

A product of the African diaspora of the Caribbean and the U.S., I was born in 1951 to unmarried parents. This ethnic mix of African immigrants shaped my village experiences.

One of my earliest memories was seeing the Atlantic Ocean for the first time.

Riding on my uncle's shoulders, I said, "What's dat I hear?"

"You'll see it soon."

I was about five years old when my Uncle Gogo carried me to the beach. I heard the ocean waves from a distance. As we walked closer, I saw the ocean on the horizon. The sight and sound of the Atlantic left me speechless. I could not fully understand what I was experiencing, but every sense was engaged. The power and vastness of the Atlantic Ocean influenced my view of the world.

I attended the Ellen Mills Scarborough Kindergarten with my cousin, Berline. We were taught by Mrs. Rebecca Chesson and Ms. Senora Outland, who were relatives of my grandmother. I learned to read from the *Royal Primer*, a booklet used to teach two-letter words like "so" and "go." Most families were related by blood or marriage. They owned the land on which they lived. This extended communal family supported my early education and development.

For my first seven years of life, I lived with my grandmother while my mother looked for employment. Moving nine miles away to Monrovia, the capital of Liberia, took me away from my cousins and our playtime in my grandmother's yard. Most people in Monrovia were renters like us, who did not own land.

I was dazzled by Monrovia and its bustling urban life. The movies shown at the Gabriel Cinema fascinated me. Tarzan and Roy Rogers movies were my favorites. Tarzan, King of the Jungle, commanded animals to assist and protect him. He single-handedly defeated a group of Africans who were scared of him and his ability to swing from vine to vine.

Roy Rogers, a singing cowboy who rode a horse, had fist fights and shoot-outs. I wanted to be a "hero" like them. I played in make-believe bars while sitting on make-believe horses in a construction site during recess.

I said to my friend, Jimmy, "Let's go and duke in the bar."

Swinging on vines was difficult to recreate in this urban setting. However, I wanted to be Tarzan, so at times, I carried a knife to school.

I sat in a packed classroom with about twenty-five boys at St. Patrick Elementary. As a third grader, I drew my knife in a school fight. The other student grabbed a broken bottle to defend himself and we fought with our respective weapons. A by-standing student was wounded in the head with the broken bottle. Blood gushed from the gash. I ran home. Jimmy, who witnessed the fight, followed me.

Following "day" school, I attended evening school with Mr. Ross in Mambi Point, Cooper Farm. My single mother wanted to keep me occupied and off the streets so I spent all day in school in the second and third grades. This regimen made me resent the confinement of the classroom. I longed for freedom. I ended up on the streets of Monrovia as a "grona" or delinquent child.

In the third grade, I was flogged before the entire school for sharing a picture of a woman's vagina with classmates. I found the medical illustration in the trash of the neighborhood pharmacy. The public punishment and label as the worst student pushed me to the streets and beaches of Monrovia.

I skipped school to experience the dazzle and "freedom" of urban life. I met with other boys and girls who skipped school. We played football—referred to as soccer in America—at Coconut Plantation, Rock Crusher, and Public

Health Pool. We picked coconuts and almonds from trees for lunch. We bathed in the Atlantic Ocean and played in the streets. Some days, I sat for hours on the J.J. Roberts Monument which stood on the tallest hill in Monrovia. From that vantage point, I watched people and vehicles moving throughout the city. I imagined being in those cars and places. My preference for street life caused me to repeat the fourth grade…twice.

During my escape from school, I became one of the grona boys of Monrovia. As children with little parental supervision, we hustled to survive. We stole food from supermarkets or ate discarded chicken bones from the garbage. We took toys and balls left unattended in people's yards. Some of us slept in unfinished buildings, on rocks, and beaches. I was fortunate to have a home to return to every day. I learned from grona boys that escape from school and parents was not freedom, but a symptom of neglect and abuse. Like many of my new friends, I was abused in the Catholic school and because my mother worked long hours to provide for us, we were often left to fend for ourselves, a byproduct of neglect.

I popped into school on occasion and discovered my father's poetry in a literature class. I knew him as a Liberian government official but did not know he was a writer. The book we read was *Poems of Liberia: 1836-1961*. This discovery sparked my interest in African poetry and drama.

Exposure to African literature was the catalyst for my academic turnaround. Another reason was an American textbook that stated, "African savages eat caterpillars." Our embarrassed fifth-grade teacher explained that this is how some Americans viewed us.

After promotion from the fifth grade, I asked my parents to send me to a boarding school to get away from the distractions of the city. In 1964, I went to Ricks Institute, a Baptist co-ed boarding school sixteen miles from Monrovia. I learned to swim, date girls, and play basketball. I was the best student in sixth grade. This environment helped shape my identity by allowing me to study and live with Africans from Cameroon, Congo, Sudan, and Nigeria.

My exposure to African literature extended beyond school curriculum. When I read *Things Fall Apart* by Chinua Achebe, it sparked a light that led me out of the darkness of self-doubt. The novel spoke to me about my resistance to American colonization. I immersed in African traditional culture and sought novels to increase my understanding of Africa's past and present.

In the eleventh grade, I became president of the drama club at Ricks and was voted "Best Actor" in the only play I ever acted. Inspired by the African Liberation and Black Power Movements of the 1960s, I wrote my first poem, "The Black Spark". I entered an oratory contest and won second place.

The Black Spark

You say you are Black
But I have a doubt
You have the guts
To say it aloud.

You say you are proud
But you have lost yourself
On the white altar of neglect
And cultural captivity.

Reclaim your heritage
Kings and Queens of Africa
And make history and civilization again.

This poem is about youth blindness to Black pride and history. This "blindness" is evident when you consider that White people cannot own land in Liberia or become citizens; however, the country remains one of the poorest and most corrupt nations in the world. Like Haiti, Liberia has been made an "inferior" nation by the global system of White supremacy.

Graduating from Ricks Institute in 1971, I returned to Monrovia to attend the University of Liberia (UL) as a science major. At UL, I volunteered with the Urban Youth Council, composed of college students. I felt a calling to become a psychologist.

I told my mother about my desire.

She said, "So you want to invoke spirits?" She saw African psychology as a part of spirituality and occult.

I was shocked at her reasoning and pondered her question without replying. I knew that psychology was the study of mind and behavior, but I could not explain exactly what psychologists did for a living. I was determined to learn.

I was asked to head the vocational guidance and counseling program at the Urban Youth Council, which later became the Federation of Liberian Youth (FLY). With no formal training in psychology, I worked with peers to assist urban youth. For about eighteen months, I counseled high school students, managed a hostel for the homeless, and ran a vacation jobs program. My volunteer work at the Urban Youth Council exposed me to activists, government officials and diplomats interested in helping youth challenged with poverty and neglect.

Since the university didn't offer psychology courses, I looked for a way to travel out of Liberia to earn a psychology degree.

Brother John, a Catholic clergyman from Louisville, Kentucky, was a member of the advisory board of the Urban Youth Council. He said, "What do you want to do with your life?"

"I want to be a psychologist."

He gave me a catalogue of Berea College in Eastern Kentucky. "If you get accepted at Berea, you can earn a bachelor's degree in psychology through a work-study program."

I applied and was accepted.

July 1973, I arrived in Dayton, OH in route to Berea. Through the Urban Youth Council, a family agreed to host me as I acclimated to American culture. I searched for Black faces to ease my fear of the unknown. During my stay, I visited Thomas Johnson (TJ) in Cincinnati, a friend from St. Patrick, where I met two Liberians, Charles and Tarpeh Roberts, who were star players of the professional soccer team, Cincinnati Comets. That evening, we went to a nightclub. Miatta Fahnbulleh, an internationally known Liberian singer, entertained us. An unexpected welcome to America.

TJ and I worked for the Appalachian Outreach program at Berea. He ran for president of the student government, and I was his campaign manager. We lost the election to an African student from Kenya.

I read my first psychology textbook and completed the introduction to psychology. I did well in my studies but struggled to make sense of American psychology and culture. The myths of Tarzan and Roy Rogers made American psychology seem unrealistic.

Ethiopia was ravaged with famine in 1974, which caused the African students to organize to raise awareness and funds for the country. This focus on Africa led to the establishment of an African Students Association (ASA) at Berea. My interest in the Black Power Movement led me to join the Black Students Union (BSU). I became its president in 1975. BSUs promoted cultural and political awareness and leadership development for African Americans at White colleges and universities. My work with African Americans in the BSU introduced me to Black psychology; a psychology of confronting anti-Black racism.

My interest in Black psychology grew as I tried to understand African American views of the world. I did my senior psychology research on racial differences. This research led me to the works of Cheikh Anta Diop, an African (Senegalese) historian and scientist. Diop's Pan-African theory and research influenced my vision of African psychology. I completed my bachelor's degree in 1976 and moved to Cincinnati, Ohio to look for a job.

I earned a Liberian government scholarship to enroll in the graduate clinical psychology program of Xavier University in Cincinnati. The training led to an internship at Longview State Mental Hospital where I met Deborah Council, a social worker. She had just moved from New York and her big-city style and attitude caught my attention. She shared my passion of working with people affected by long-term mental illnesses.

In 1979, I transferred to the University of Cincinnati (UC) to pursue a doctorate in educational psychology to better understand the chronic mental illnesses I was confronted with at Longview State.

Deborah and I dated for about five years while I completed my doctorate degree, and she completed her master's in social work. We married in 1984.

My advanced degree did not guarantee a job in higher education. I ended up job hunting in Atlanta, Georgia. To make ends meet, I worked for two months as a day laborer, packing boxes and mowing lawns at a warehouse. Depressed and with increased self-doubt, I went to several interviews for college teaching positions.

Deborah said, "No one will hire you with those dreadlocks."

While studying for my doctorate degree, I was introduced to Rastafari. Symbolic of my changing lifestyle and value system, I let my hair grow into dreads. The seed of doubt she planted grew with each job rejection.

Catharine Harris, a colleague who edited my dissertation, said, "You not landing a job has nothing to do with your hair. You are not confident in these interviews. You have skills as a researcher and instructor. If they do not hire you, then take your skills and experience somewhere else."

Her brief lecture gave me a different way to describe my skills and experience. My next interview was at Ferris State University in Big Rapids, Michigan. Prepared and confident, I was hired as a visiting psychology professor. In 1986, I began full-time employment as a professor of psychology.

I set a goal of being the "best psychology professor" in the U.S. At the end of the school year, students nominated me as the best new professor at Ferris State. This demonstrated to me that I needed to set high goals to achieve excellence.

I was asked to participate in a celebration of Black history and arts as the new professor on campus. For my first public reading, I read one of my father's poems, "We Can Do It, You and I". Three students read his other poems: "No Longer Yesterday", "You Ask Me", and "Because You Told Me". In *We Can Do It You and I*, H. Cary Thomas described "The African's United States" as a song—derived from the "trail of black-skinned warriors"—that the world must hear. He cautioned that the dream may seem far-fetched; however, if we fail to build "a mighty, mighty, state...where our fathers lived and died," it will bring "shame and mockery" to our race. The title of this poem became the theme of the Black History Month program at Ferris State University in 1987.

In 1987, I went to Denison University in Ohio as a visiting psychology professor to be closer to Deborah and our sons, Emman and Dakona, in Cincinnati.

My confidence in psychology grew. This experience led me to apply and get offers from two institutions. I accepted the position at Sinclair Community College in Dayton, Ohio. In just two years, I moved from being a laborer to a tenure-track professor.

Teaching African American Psychology was a significant milestone in my journey as a psychologist. For the first time, I felt I was doing what I came to America to do: African psychology.

During the same period, I became involved with efforts to end the Liberian Civil War. In 1990, I traveled to Liberia to rescue my mother who had suffered a stroke. She resided behind the frontline of Charles Taylor's National Patriotic Front of Liberia. My experience was reported in a 1991 article in *Dayton Daily News; Sons Help Their Mom Escape War: Woman Caught Behind Liberian Rebel Lines*. Seeing my family and friends trapped in a war-torn environment was traumatic. Tears rolled down my face when my mother walked through the morning mist out of captivity. The stench of rotting bodies filled the air of Monrovia. Battle scarred.

When I returned to the U.S., my mother followed a month later. I worked with other Liberians to establish the Dayton Area Liberian Association. Founded in 1992, this organization assisted Liberian women and children who were victims of the Liberian Civil War.

I planned and hosted the first Liberian Studies Conference at Sinclair Community College in 1995. International scholars traveled to Dayton to discuss Liberia for three days. At the keynote address by Dr. Amos Sawyer, some Liberians verbally attacked the former interim President of Liberia for corruption. I got on the stage with Dr. Sawyer, to minimize the verbal attack against him. He eventually fielded questions about his tenure in office.

The All-Liberian Conference was established to assist in ending the Liberian Civil War. In 1996, I was invited to speak on the effect of the war on Liberia's education and development at a vocational education conference in Chennai, India. I discovered that African communities in Asia were established before slavery.

I went on a Fulbright study-tour of Southern Africa in 2003. As a member of the Midwest International Studies Institute, we visited Botswana, Eswatini, and South Africa. I developed a deeper understanding of Southern Africa and included this knowledge in my African American Studies courses. I learned that Africans in the South saw themselves more like African Americans than West Africans.

For the second time, my colleagues in the Sinclair Psychology Department encouraged me to apply for the chairperson position. Unlike the first time, I felt ready to lead. In 2008, I was selected as chairperson of psychology and coordinator of Africana Studies. This position allowed me to merge my practice and research in African psychology. I served as chairperson for nine years and retired from Sinclair in 2018. I returned to Monrovia in March 2019 to build a house in Brewerville.

Chapter 2

Self-Knowledge

"To know animals is good.
To know trees is good.
To know oneself is better
Than them all."
—Mende Proverb

Knowledge of oneself is the basis of all other knowledge. However, the trauma of colonization, enslavement, and civil wars has brought darkness upon us. In a world dominated by anti-Black racism, capitalism, and technology, we have become blinded.

After returning from war-torn Liberia in 1991, I asked myself, "Why all this fighting and destruction? Who turned us against one another? Where did this envy and greed originate?"

To answer these questions, I studied the work of Cedric X (Clark) and others who suggested that African psychology is rooted in ancient human thought and self-realization. Many ideas found in modern science and philosophy originated in the Nile Valley, Congo, and Niger River civilizations of which Kemet (Egypt) is the most famous.

The idea that humans originated from and are sustained by water is retold in many creation stories of African civilizations. Up to 60% of the body of an adult human is water. The brain and heart are composed of 73% water, according to H. H. Mitchell.[1] Water is the most valued resource. African nations depend on rivers, seas, and oceans. Global warming is threatening Africans' survival. An awareness that the environment is being destroyed by technological pollution and capitalist exploitation has led to climate change policies in Africa.[2]

In 1986, Wade W. Nobles, former president of the Association of Black Psychologists, said that the roots of human psychology and African psychology can be found in creation stories told in the Nile Valley.[3] One story of Ptah states that the universe was created through the power of mind or thought. The *Shabaka/Stone Old Kingdom Text 2780-2260 BC* suggests that Ptah exists through "every divine word and thought," which occupies everybody. Everything that exists must first be conceived by a living mind. Ptah is a symbol of the mind.

I chose to become a psychologist in high school, but I had to speak this desire into existence and take action. I read African literature and tried to better understand African culture which was absent in my high school curriculum.

In 1969, my social studies teacher, Mr. Osei, recognized my interest in social matters. He gave me a book, *Towns in Africa*, as an academic award. As my first book on Africa's social science, I have carried this book in my personal library for almost fifty years.

In 1986, Wade Nobles wrote, "African psychology today

---

[1] Mitchell, H.H. "Water in You." Journal of Biological Chemistry, Vol.158, no.2, 1945. P. 537.

[2] "Acemoglu, Daron. "Comments and Discussion". *Brookings Papers on Economic Activity*, Vol. 2020, no. 2, 2020. (p.p. 432-443).

[3] Nobles, Wade W. *African Psychology: Toward Its Reclamation, Reascension or Revitalization*. Institute for the Advanced Study of Black Family Life and Culture, 1986.

has gone unrecognized and misunderstood because of our inability to understand the role of symbolism in the African mind—both ancient and modern."[4] The use of symbols and symbolism in African psychology and literature can be viewed as creative representations of spiritual qualities and the development of our divinity.

The creation stories of the Nile Valley, Niger, and Congo River civilizations teach science and philosophy to current and future generations. In African psychology, using Western languages and books are major obstacles to understand African thought and behavior. This cultural domination leads to the destruction and falsification of African knowledge and sciences. Hollywood movies have played a significant role in promoting White cultural domination. Diop discovered this discrepancy in his study of ancient Africa, especially Egypt. Euro-American and Arab scholars deliberately destroyed, stole, and mutilated ancient African artifacts, symbols, and inventions to claim supremacy over African humanity and divinity.

In the 1960s, African psychology reasserted itself as a part of the African Liberation Struggle for political independence and Black Power. This liberation of African psychology by Black scholars was based on the recognition that Western psychology and social sciences failed to give an accurate understanding of African life and self-consciousness.

In the early 1960s, African Heads of States convened in Monrovia to form the Organization of African Unity (OAU) now known as the African Union. The reconception of Africa was mapped out before my youthful eyes. This

---

[4] Nobles, Wade W. *African Psychology: Toward Its Reclamation, Reascension or Revitalization*. Institute for the Advanced Study of Black Family Life and Culture, 1986.

movement inspired me.

The 1968 founding of the Association of Black Psychologists marked this separation from a Euro-American version of African thought and behavior toward the reclamation of African self-determination.

At the University of Liberia, I discovered the ideas of Edward W. Blyden, the 19th-century scholar and educator who helped establish the Liberian College, which became the University of Liberia. In his classic work, *African Life and Customs* (1908), he suggested that the African personality was more cooperative, collective, and spiritual than what he saw as the rampant individualism, materialism, and competitiveness of the European personality. I wrote pages of Blyden's ideas and quotes and carried them with me.

Psychology was originally the study of the soul (psyche means soul; ology means study). However, Euro-American psychology shifted the focus to a study of behavior and mental processes, which introduced darkness and self-doubt in African thought and behavior.

African philosophy suggests that the essence of life is spirit and light. Spirit is both symbolic and reality. African psychology is the study of the human soul/spirit traveling in spiritual and material universes. This field of study involves every aspect of life: scientific, spiritual, social, economic, and artistic ways of being and becoming African.

Euro-American scientists recently came to understand that 95% of the universe is "dark matter" and "dark energy" (spirit) which are unknown and immeasurable.[5] This advancement in physics suggests that African Spirit is present and integrated in all aspects of human culture and

---

[5] Cottell, Geoff. "Dark Matter and Dark Energy." *Matter: A Short Introduction,* 2019, pp.132-142.

life. It is in our DNA.

Western psychology's focus on materialism and objectivity is narrow. It does not account for spirit and symbols which are at the core of African psychology. Since Western technology cannot measure spirit like brain activity and behaviors; it assumes that it does not exist.

African psychology is scientifically diverse and complex. In 1982, W. Curtis Banks suggested that African psychology can be understood in terms of its critical method, judgment, and acceptance of ideas when compared to Euro-American psychology.[6] This approach uses three critical methods: deconstruction, reconstruction, and construction.

Deconstruction in African Psychology

A deconstructionist approach represents Black scientists' rejection of "facts" and theories of Euro-American psychology as useful tools to understand African people. It rejects the darkness of White supremacy by spotlighting its lies and manipulations. Since discovering Diop's work on ancient Africa, I deconstructed the theories and findings in American psychology. I rejected the "history" that philosophy and medicine began in Greek civilization. Instead, I learned and taught that the origin of psychology is not in Greece or Germany but Ancient Egypt. The foundations and medical research from which modern psychology drew its inspiration and methods have their roots in Africa. The first recorded psychological experiment occurred in Egypt around 700 BC. [7]

---

[6] Banks, W. Curtis. Stanford University, unpublished manuscripts, 1982.
[7] Mohamed, Wael M. Y. "Psychology International Newsletter", Mar. 2012.

Teaching research methods, I insisted that students understood that the researcher constructs operational definition from personal experience to organize behavior and mental processes into measurable units. Researchers impose definition on events that appear to be chaotic and disorganized. European psychologists measured intelligence by defining it as intelligence quotient (IQ) or analytical thinking identifying differences.

When explained to Kpelle rice farmers in Liberia, this analytical way of thinking was deemed "stupid." The farmers saw relational thinking as more intelligent than analytical thinking because it is group-oriented with emphasis on performance; whereas, analytical thinking is individualistic and reflective. This study demonstrated that culture shapes thoughts and values.

Another example of shining a light on the darkness of White supremacy occurred in the Black Student Union (BSU) at Berea. In 1975, some BSU students volunteered with the theater department to do a Black version of Shakespeare's *MacBeth* for Black History Month. I rejected the idea that African Americans should imitate Europeans in matters of our history and culture. I suggested that we do something original and focused on Black history. After some resistance, we created an original program that involved major artistic events in Black history and most of the young, gifted, and Black students in the BSU.

Analytical research of racial differences was the focus of my senior research at Berea. I wanted to understand the differences I observed in Eastern Kentucky. My findings and conclusion rejected Moynihan's notion that African Americans were defective Black versions of White Americans. His infamous 1965 *Moynihan Report* concluded that "the Negro family" was falling apart when compared to

White families. I demonstrated that systematic differences between Black and White students' pattern recognition could be explained by different cultural experiences.

This idea of different cultural experiences being misunderstood as cognitive deficits was reexamined by Asa Hilliard's (1981) research *IQ as Catechism: Ethic and Cultural Bias or Invalid Science*. Utilizing the standard requirements for evaluating scientific research, he found that IQ tests used in public schools were invalid. This misuse of IQ tests as the primary tool for placing and tracking Black and Latino students in public schools was rejected by the Association of Black Psychologists and banned by a presiding judge in California.

As a psychologist intern, I had to administer IQ tests, personality assessments, and projective tests to patients in Longview State Mental Hospital. The accuracy of these tests was questionable even for White patients, who were often on antipsychotic medication. This use of psychological testing to diagnose mental illness was not scientific when it applied to Africans. However, they provided analytical support to my clinical judgment and diagnosis.

I ran into problems using psychological testing for research with African students. My justification for using these tests was not grounded in cultural validity, but my assumption that this option was the only means to measure African students' personalities. This type of cultural domination makes African scientific research difficult. I was trapped in this darkness until another African student questioned the cultural validity of this method. Reminded that the tools and definitions of American psychologists were not the same for African scientists, I rejected psychological testing as a way of measuring and defining African thought and behavior. Instead, I used interviews and field research methods to describe the African experience in the U.S.

Reconstruction in African Psychology

A reconstructionist approach involves correcting the errors and lies of Euro-American psychology by applying a more relevant and useful tool to deal with African development. My practice in African psychology shined a light on the roots of psychology by highlighting human migration and development in and out of Africa.

One of the first articles I published on African American education advocated for the incorporation of African culture and history in American public education. I argued that the lack of African values, languages, and contributions increased African students' failures and dropout rates. This article contributed to a discussion on the endangered Black male. I became the educational consultant of the independent Black primary school, W.E.B. Du Bois Academy of Dayton in 1990.

This elementary school was funded by an Ohio grant to reduce alcohol and drug use among African American youth. The public education curriculum was revised by incorporating African-centered rituals and rites of passage. Implementing the revision reduced alcohol and drug use among these youth, and gaps in their academic achievements on the Ohio State Grade Equivalency Tests. However, the curriculum was poorly funded. Most teachers and community supporters were not fully committed to Pan-African values and perspectives.

I turned on other sources of light by advocating for the creation of an African American Studies program at Sinclair Community College. I founded and coordinated African

American Studies in 1993. I used existing courses taught in other academic programs and created two new ones: Introduction to African American Studies and African American Psychology. This new program was used to recruit and retain African and African American students at Sinclair.

The program was underfunded and marginalized by the college. However, I supplemented students' educations with the African American Culture Club and Alliance for Black Leadership and Education (ABLE) Youth Training Institute. I used these extra-curricular student organizations to train students in community organizing and leadership. Most of the students who participated in these organizations maintained their commitments to self-determination and African empowerment. This introduction of African values and history assisted hundreds of students to reconstruct their lives and sense of self.

This approach of implementing new sources of light also occurred in my spiritual development when I embraced Rastafari. My birth name is Winston Emmanuel Thomas. When I became a professor, I used W. Emmanuel Thomas as my official name. I had another change when I became Rastafari. I felt at home in the Rasta community of Cincinnati, which was composed of college dropouts, delinquent youth, and social misfits like the grona boys from Monrovia.

My walk toward Zion and Pan-Africanism became "irie" (pronounced eye-ree, it's Jamaican for cool), and "upfull" (upright) within this collective. I met friends at the University of Cincinnati (UC) who had identified themselves as Black Hebrew Israelites but moved toward Rastas.

I attended The Black Man's Think Tank first held at UC

in 1983. This conference brought top Black male scholars to speak to the university and community. Maulana Karenga, Na'im Akbar, Molefi K. Asante, and Kwame Ture were some of the speakers who had reconstructed themselves and changed their names. Their example inspired me to reclaim my African name of Boikai Sellassie Twe. Boikai, which means helper in God's work, originated from the Vai ethnic mix of my hometown. Sellassie identified me with the Pan-African vision of Rastafari and Twe was the neighborhood where I grew up near New Kru Town.

To explain identity reconstruction, William Cross suggested a theory of Negrescence, the Negro-to-Black conversion. One of the most researched reconstructionist theories in African psychology, explained that negroes go through five stages to develop their racial identity of being Black or African.

In 1993, Janet Helms reconstructed this five-stage theory as follows:[8]

1. Pre-Encounter. An orientation toward White culture and away from Black/African culture. Most Africans are educated by Europeans and Arabs and take on their identities and names. As a child, I wanted to be Tarzan, the White king of the jungle.
2. Dissonance. Individuals encounter events that shatter self-perception and views of being Black/African. The African Liberation and Black Power Movements were catalysts in this phase of deconstruction.
3. Immersion and Emersion. This stage involves a new way of thinking and incorporates being

---

[8] Helms, Janet E. *Black and White Racial Identity: Theory, Research and Practice.* Praeger, 1993.

Black/African. African literature and psychology provide new ways of being African in this phase of reconstruction.
4. Internalization. The individual has internalized a new identity and is more flexible and tolerant of other cultural groups. This growth is seen in the African Union where many different cultural groups work together for mutual survival and development.
5. Internalization-Commitment. The individual possesses the characteristics of the internalization stage and works for the liberation of all oppressed people. As the most oppressed people in the world, Africans work to liberate ourselves and other oppressed people. This commitment involves the construction of Pan-African institutions and a going to Zion, a physical and spiritual journey to righteousness. The Negrescence Theory suggests that African people are reconstructing their identity as they move to well-being and truth-justice.

Construction in African Psychology

The constructionist approach reflects the view that psychologists must work to promote the welfare of Black/African people and advance new self-knowledge. This approach lets sunlight drive away the darkness of self-doubt and fear.

In 1991, Na'im Akbar argued that religious and cultural beliefs are critical to any constructive understanding of Black behaviors. He stressed the role of naturalness, spirituality, and human connection to the forces of the universe (dark matter and dark energy). Akbar constructed a new way to define mental disorders and mental health among Black populations. He identified mental health as the intentional identification and commitment to one's African identity.[9]

I used Akbar's theory of mental disorders to help understand the darkness faced during the Liberian Civil War (1989-2003). In *A Perspective on Psychological Disorders in Liberia* published in *Liberian Studies Journal* in 1994, I argued that Liberians were engaged in self destruction due to their lack of intentional identification with their African heritage. Liberians have identified more with America (Babylon) and less with Africa (Zion). I followed that article with *A Review of African Psychology in West Africa*. In this 1998 publication in *Liberian Studies Journal*, I discussed the crisis faced by Liberia and Sierra Leone. I suggested construction of national identities based on African culture and religion and less on the darkness of enslavement and colonization.

I hosted the Peace and Reconciliation Workshop following the 1995 Liberian Studies Association Conference. This workshop contributed to the creation of the All Liberian Conference (ALC) of which I served as general secretary. This nationalist organization sent a delegate, Marcus Dahn, to the Liberian Peace Conference in Accra, Ghana which led to the Accra Peace Accord. This peace accord ended the first phase of the Liberian Civil War and led to national elections in 1997. In 1998, I published another article in *Liberian Studies Journal. Asili of Liberian Psychology* examined the psychological imbalance that led to the civil war. In this work, I proposed that Liberians study and use African

---

[9] Akbar, Na'im. "Mental Disorders among African Americans". In R.L. Jones (Ed.), *Black Psychology*. (p.p. 339-352). Cobb & Henry. 1991.

culture to construct a national identity and Liberian psychology.

The Abuja Peace Accord ended the second phase of the Liberian Civil War. Liberia was heading to national elections. I presented a paper on the psychology of Liberian leadership at the LSA Conference in Lansing, Michigan. J. Emmanuel Bowier, former Minister of Culture and Information of Liberia and colleague, encouraged me to create a pamphlet to promote voters' educations before the 2005 general elections. I self-published a booklet, *Which Way Liberia: The Gun or the Book?*, and sent it to William Allen, Minister of Culture and Information of Liberia, for distribution.

In this booklet, I had two essays, *The Crisis in West African Leadership: Liberian Trials and Tribulations* and *Edward Wilmot Blyden's Lessons in African Psychology*. This work was my contribution to the successful elections that led Ellen Johnson-Sirleaf to become the first female head of state in modern Africa. Without hard evidence, Minister Allen told me that it made a contribution.

The three approaches are not distinctive categories of research and practice but suggest ways of understanding and explaining revolutionary shifts from accepted thinking in psychology.

Chapter 3

Blackness - Melanin Magic

"The lover sees the smoothness of the woman's skin. The doctor sees the illness hidden under it."
—North African Proverb

My understanding of blackness in African psychology first came in high school when I read some of my father's poems and wrote "The Black Spark" (See page 17).

A greater understanding of psychological blackness came when I read the writings of Edward Wilmot Blyden. In 1878, he wrote, "The European world is, as yet, only in the infancy of its studies in African psychology. No European statesmen or philanthropist has, yet, even attempted to grapple with it. Far more difficult of settlement than sources of the Nile, the intellectual character and susceptibility of the Negro will probably, for ages yet, elude the grasp and comprehension of the most sagacious European." He concluded, "Only the Negro will be able to explain the Negro to the rest of mankind."[10]

Africans' victories over the French in the Haitian Revolution of 1791-1804 and Italians at Adowa in Ethiopia in 1896 led Blyden to question European claims of

---

[10] Blyden, Edward W. *Christianity, Islam and the Negro Race*. Black Classic Press. Baltimore, MD. 1878.

superiority over Africans' intelligence, characters, and self-determination. Blyden was also a critic of mixed-race Africans about their lack of allegiance to African sovereignty and blackness. Some scholars saw the claim as promoting Black supremacy and exclusion. Black supremacy has been a radical view in African thought that sought to confront global White supremacy by pointing to truth and justice. This positive psychology of blackness is seen by some of today's scholars as cultural nationalism.

My desire to be African and self-determined led me to embrace and celebrate the Black Power Movement of my childhood. The attack on White supremacy and elevation of blackness were evident in the Harlem Renaissance of the 1920s and Black Arts Movement in the 1960s and 1970s. Both of these Black literature movements have been accused of supporting Black supremacy because of their confrontation to White supremacy. The Harlem Renaissance influenced the Civil Rights Movement of the 1950s and the poetry of my father. In contrast, the Black Arts Movement influenced the Black Power Movement and my writing and practice of psychology.

Research at the Berea College Library introduced me to scientific evidence of the erasure of blackness found in Cheikh Anta Diop's research. Using Egyptian mummies, Diop demonstrated that ancient Egyptians were Black and never represented themselves as Indo-Europeans or Asians. He argued that even though the notion of race is relative, molecular biology has isolated racial markers which are exclusively found in each racial group. After measuring the percentage of melanin in the mummies and comparing the images of ancient Egyptians, Diop used objective methods to conclude that Ramses II, Seti I, and Thutmose III were Black men.

Diop wrote that "Africa should, on controversial matters, access the truth by its own intellectual investigation, maintain itself to this truth until humanity knows that Africa will not be frustrated anymore."[11] This spark brought light to the darkness of European and Arab lies about Black inferiority.

Further investigation into the psychology of blackness led me to the article, *Voodoo or I.Q.: An Introduction to African Psychology* by Cedric X (Clark) and others (1975). These Black psychologists argued that African psychology is material and spiritual, Blacks are not inferior to Whites, the self is connected to other selves and the environment, and Black people and White people cannot be measured by the same yardstick in terms of behavior.

They further suggested that the African race is evolutionarily more advanced than Caucasians and is the original source of genetic factors that account for contemporary White and Black behavior. This group of Black psychologists argued that intelligence needed to be redefined and directly related to the presence of melanin in the human genetic makeup.

Scholars, like Diop, suggested that African intellectual investigations should challenge the White minority who sought to establish the standards of truth and justice as being "White." I raised this issue in my dissertation research about the miseducation and disorientation faced by African college students in U.S. colleges. These "White" standards and "truths" imposed on Africa and Africans contribute to the "inferiority" and corruption in African leadership and institutions. This systematic erasure of African blackness

---

[11] Diop, Cheikh A. *The African Origin of Civilization: Myth or Reality*. Lawrence Hill, Chicago. 1974.

and cultures threatens African development and survival.

In 1970, Psychiatrist Frances Cress Welsing advanced a controversial social psychological theory on blackness by focusing on whiteness and its strategies for genetic survival. She asked questions about the psychological nature of oppressive Whites. She concluded that White supremacy is an offensive drive for superiority or domination due to a deep and pervading sense of inadequacy and inferiority observed among racist Whites, like former President Donald Trump, White evangelicals, and White gun lovers.[12]

According to Welsing, whiteness or blackness is not only due to culture and social conditioning but also the genetic ability to produce sufficient amounts of melanin; the ink of life.[13] She proposed that Whites are melanin deficient which leads to self-hate and alienation. This deficiency has caused them to develop an elaborate system of domination and lies. This global system is used to manipulate Blacks and other people of color into accepting White supremacy. This theory, though rejected by some scholars, has created a deeper understanding of blackness and the roles of melanin in intelligence, consciousness, memory, psychic awareness, and learning ability and White supremacy's attempt to misdirect them.

This theory helped me understand why Whites and Arabs have battled for control of our minds, lands, and resources. They sought to exclude us from wealth and power even though melanin gave us both. In the cases of South Africa and Brazil, White minorities and their "negro"

---

[12] Welsing, Francis C. "The Cress Theory of Color-Confrontation." *Black Scholar*, 5 (8), 32-40, 1974.
[13] Barnes, Carol. *Melanin: The Key to Black Greatness: The Harmful Effects of Toxic Drugs on Melanin Centers within Black Humans.* Lushena. 2001.

partners continue to control the majority Black populations and their resources. This social theory also helps to explain why Liberia has remained a neo-colonial state under the control of the U.S./Babylon for 175 years.

In his book, *Melanin: The Chemical Key to Black Greatness*, Carol Barnes suggests that melanin is a unique biopolymer or "life chemical" found in high concentrations in various organs in Black humans. He wrote that melanin is responsible for manufacturing and sustaining life. Beyond being responsible for skin color, it is located in the central nervous system, autonomic nervous system, peripheral nervous system, diffuse neuro endocrine system, and viscera. Melanin is also found in soil, plants, animals, creeks, lakes, springs, seas, and rivers. He wrote, "Melanin is Black simply because its chemical structure will not allow any type of energy to escape once that energy has come in contact with its structure."[14]

He further suggested that melanin can be viewed as a partially charged battery that captures energy from light and sounds. Black humans can charge their melanin by being in the sun, or proximity to other energy sources, or the right musical sounds. He also suggested that Black humans can damage melanin by taking harmful drugs.

Diop, Cress-Welsing, X (Clark), and Barnes argue that melanin is a civilizing chemical responsible for the existence of civilization, philosophy, religion, truth, justice, and righteousness. Black humans are able to experience the world at a constantly "higher energy state" than what is experienced by non-Black humans. Black people shape Black cultures to reflect a "higher energy state" than those

---

[14] Barnes, Carol. *Melanin: The Key to Black Greatness: The Harmful Effects of Toxic Drugs on Melanin Centers within Black Humans*. Lushena. 2001.

designed by non-Blacks. This observation is reflected in African dances, attire, cooking, and more.

I introduced my students to this African view that celebrates melanin magic. The Black Power Conferences of the 1960s defined blackness by focusing on the three Cs of blackness: color, consciousness, and culture. I exposed my students and community to melanin's role in blackness.

In 1992, Psychologist Kobi Kambon suggested that Africans who were enslaved and colonized suffered from moderate to severe forms of "psychological/cultural misorientation." Also referred to as cultural and moral blindness, he proposed that White supremacy led to the miseducation of Africans and an anti-African orientation which led to the premise of an "inferior" African. He pointed out that independent African institutions are few, unpopular, and poorly supported. In the area of religion, Africans accept and practice White supremacy as the core of religious beliefs and activities.

Africans also accept and practice White cultural domination in economic and business activities. They accept White supremacy through dependency on Euro-American media, patronage, and affirmation. They permit the names and physical characteristics of Whites and Arabs to dominate self-imagery/self-definition. They accept and utilize anti-African inaction toward social/racial empowerment. Kambon also wrote that Africans require Euro-American acknowledgement, recognition, and approval in all areas of life. They live in the shadows of inferiority and death from White supremacy. Kambon recommended African liberation and well-being by doing the following:[15]

1. Massive reeducation toward a Pan-African Nationalist consciousness/identity. African groupings throughout the diaspora must see themselves as African Nations.
2. The African community must remove or eliminate Eurocentric cultural icons/symbols from the home, school, and natural environments of African reality.
3. Non-African names must be eliminated from our African reality to reclaim our optimal African mental health.
4. Return to a belief in and practice of African-centered religions and the institutionalization of traditional African spiritual systems.
5. The African community must institute life-cycle rituals, holydays/holiday rituals, and establish sacred symbols and shrines to commemorate sacred African events and conditions.

---

[15] Kambon, Kobi K.K. *The African Personality in America*. Nubian Nation. 1992.

Chapter 4

Black Migration and Repatriation

"We see a new Ethiopia, a new Africa, stretching her hands of influence throughout the world, teaching man the way of life and peace, the way to God."
— Marcus Garvey

Africans are the original migrants of the world. We migrated before history was recorded. The Out of Africa theory suggests that we, the first humans, traveled to all the continents and islands of the world. It is difficult to speculate why we migrated out of Africa. From history, we know some migrations were forced by natural and human disasters and others were voluntary and adventurous. The first humans migrated from South and East Africa to populate the rest of Africa and the world. Most of the early migrations were searches for food and water. We continue to migrate within and outside of Africa to improve our well-being and security.

African migration is psychological and physical. I used African literature to psychologically migrate to parts of Africa and the diaspora. However, physical migration has become a political issue in Europe and America. According to some surveys, one in three Africans have considered migrating to another African country. Fewer have emigrated to Europe or America. Africans are being enslaved, exploited, and murdered as we try to migrate across Africa and beyond to improve our lives. The U.S. and Europe have closed their borders to us and other migrants looking for work to escape poverty and insecurity.

My emigration to the U.S. was voluntary and aspirational. I traveled to get training that was not available in Liberia. Many face this decision as they seek to gain skills and employment. This search for opportunities has led Africans to migrate to the four corners of the Earth and contribute to the building of nations.

The migration of Edward Wilmot Blyden, W.E.B. Du Bois, Martin R. Delany, and Alexander Crummell, founders of Pan-Africanism, from the African diaspora to West Africa shaped their consciousness and opportunities to become teachers, philosophers, politicians, and Pan-Africanists. Migration shaped their views of the unity of Africans and Black people globally. Marcus Garvey spread Pan-Africanism across the globe through the Universal Negro Improvement Association (UNIA). He developed his philosophy and vision of repatriation from his migration to Europe, South America, and the U.S. The opportunity to interact with other Africans in the diaspora also shaped his vision for the United States of Africa.

The idea of Pan-Africanism as a way to defend Africans against White supremacy in the diaspora and in Africa was developed through migration. Kwame Nkrumah, who proposed the unification of Africa in 1958, was a migrant. Some oral historians in Liberia and Ghana suggest that he was born in Liberia as Francis Weah, grew-up in Ghana, traveled, and then lived in the U.S. In New York, he was exposed to the UNIA and its vision of the United States of Africa. As the first president of Ghana, he promoted Pan-Africanism and was the driving force in establishing the Organization of African Unity in 1963.

The African Union's Protocol of Free Movement has been adopted by all fifty-five African states. In 2019, it was implemented by Ghana and Rwanda to allow free movement of Africans across the continent. This protocol was first proposed in the 1991 Abuja Treaty. The African Union passport has been issued to facilitate this freedom of movement across Africa.

Bob Marley, a musician from Jamaica, migrated to the U.S. in the 1960s. He was influenced by music and politics of the Black Power Movement. On his return to Jamaica, he wrote some of the most Black-consciousness songs of that era. His ninth studio album with the Wailers, *Exodus*, was released in June 1977. This album, which propelled him to international stardom, was recorded in London, where he migrated after a 1976 assassination attempt on his life. In the title song, "Exodus: Movement of Jah people", he sang about leaving Babylon, representative of enslavement and White supremacy, and going to Zion for an African homecoming.

This song reflects Africans' deep aspiration of psychological and physical movements toward opportunities and freedom from White supremacy (Babylon) toward the Pan-African dream of African unification.

Between 1916 and 1970, the movement of African people occurred in the U.S. during "The Great Migration." Six million African Americans left the American South and moved north to flee racism and unemployment. My wife's mother, Elsie, and her siblings migrated to New York and

Philadelphia from North Carolina in search of employment. This major transfer of African population caused African Americans to shift from being rural to mostly urban and suburban people. New challenges and opportunities arose with this migration.

The Association for the Study of African American Life and History (ASALH), founded by Carter G. Woodson, designated 2019 as the year to study Black Migration, "the movement of Africans to new destinations and new social realities." As a member of the Paul Laurence Dunbar Branch of ASALH in Dayton, I sat with Kwaku Larry Crowe for a five-hour recorded interview to capture my migration to the U.S. and return to Liberia. This interview reminded me of my paternal grandparents' repatriation to Liberia from Barbados. Also, the great-grandparents of my mother repatriated from the American South, possibly Jamestown, Virginia to Liberia. My great-grandmother, Sarah Shaw, said that she was born on May 30, 1896, on board a ship carrying her family to Liberia.

My mother, Elizabeth Flowers-Gibson, who was born in Liberia, emigrated to the U.S. in 1991 to escape the Liberian Civil War. She returned to Liberia in 2007. I returned to Monrovia in March 2019 to spend time with my mother. She died November 29, 2019.

On May 11, 2019, I attended Bob Marley Day at the Imperial Castle (a Rastafari shop and meeting place) on the South Beach of Monrovia. This celebration reminded me of the importance of migration and repatriation in Rastafari and Pan-Africanism. We remembered the Pan-African plan of Marcus Garvey to repatriate Africans from the U.S. to Liberia. We were reminded of some Rastas who walked from the U.K., a kingdom built on slavery and White supremacy, to Ethiopia, the headquarters of the African

Union.

Aspiration for a better life and spiritual growth is embedded in African psychology, to reach Zion. Another idea in African psychology related to movement is Sankofa. This act of returning to one's place of origin or retrieving one's culture and heritage is a major concern reflected in some of our songs and literature.

Recollections of origins and migrations from faraway places are noted in literature. Egyptians traveled down the Nile River from the mountains of Ethiopia and the valleys of Nubia. Africans in West Africa migrated from central and east Africa. Those from Liberia came from the Empire of Mali and Songhai in West Africa. The greatest recorded migration was the Transatlantic enslavement which took about 12-20 million Africans to Europe and the Americas. This forced migration changed the world over the past 500 years. This seizure created the industrial revolution in Europe and America and led to the colonization, division, and underdevelopment of Africa.

The creation of Liberia in 1822 by the American Colonization Society as an asylum for repatriated Africans from the U.S., highlights this concern in African psychology. Liberia was the original site chosen by Marcus Garvey and the Universal Negro Improvement Association (UNIA) in the 1920s to repatriate Africans from the Americas and the Caribbean. The Black Star Line shipping company was created to fulfill this goal. However, the U.S. government pressured Liberia to reject Garvey and UNIA's repatriation project.

Liberia played a role in the birth of Pan-Africanism by being an asylum for Joseph J. Roberts, Edward W. Blyden, and Alexander Crummell and host to Martin Delany and W.E.B. Du Bois. One of the first conferences on African unity was held in Sanniquellie, Liberia in 1959 when President W.V.S. Tubman met with Sekou Toure and Kwame Nkrumah.

My mother, five brothers, two uncles, four aunts, and a host of other relatives emigrated from Liberia to the U.S. from 1970-2004. This relocation was due to searching for skills, employment, and security from the civil crisis and war.

In April 2019, Uncle Thomas Roberts died in Providence, Rhode Island at the age of 79. Although he was buried in Providence, the family gathered in Brewerville to celebrate his life. This dispersal of African families across Africa and the world is the norm. A quarter of Africans surveyed indicated that they had a family member living in another country. Those in southern Africa had the strongest preference to stay in their region. North Africans had the strongest desire to leave for Europe and North America.[16]

Rastafari has made repatriation a central project. I fulfilled this vision of return to Africa after 46 years. In 2019, repatriation or Sankofa was promoted as "The Year of Return" in Ghana. Nigeria announced a "Door of Return" policy for 2020. These states make it easy for Africans from the diaspora to return to visit, conduct business, acquire land, and become citizens. In 2019, Ghana became the state with the fastest growing economy in Africa. Other West African states are opening borders to free movement and the return of Africans from the diaspora.

---

[16] Flahaux, Marie-L, & De Haas. "African Migration: Trends, Patterns, Drivers." *Comparative Migration Studies,* (4), 1. 2016.

Pan-Africanism is a product of Black migration and is helping to create the projects of African regional cooperation and economic integration. Pan-Africanism can also be used to prevent civil wars and displacement of Africans within the African Union.

Boikai S. Twe

Chapter 5

Lifecycle in a Village

"The fruit never falls too far from the tree."
– African proverb

My early childhood was spent with my grandmother, Mai Shaw Roberts. She was the family midwife who assisted village women to give birth.

I remember the birth of my brother, Alex. The sun was bright on that first day of August. At four years old, I banged on a zinc tub in the back of my grandmother's home.

My grandmother said, "You wan take the skin off your babe brother with da noise?"

I stopped banging. Her question notified me that I had a new brother, and my behavior could affect him. As the first of six sons, this lesson shaped my sense of responsibility for my brothers.

Like other Africans, my brother was not named at birth. The family waited two to three weeks to determine the identity of the child and to see if the child would survive. I recall a naming ceremony where the newborn was taken outside the house for the first time. Singing and celebrating the child's birth, the family circled the house several times. The umbilical cord was buried in the backyard on the hopes that the child would stay alive and not make a quick return to the spirit world.

Ma Sando, a Gola woman who was Zoe or leader of the

Sande (women) Society, lived across the street. Her yard was visited by young girls dressed in beads around their waists, arms, and necks and white chalk covering their bodies. They sang and danced as a part of the rites of passage to womanhood. They brought masked dancers, which required children younger than ten to be indoors, to avoid being "taken away" and forced into a secret initiation by the elders of Sande. These indigenous rites of passage were practiced by Gola and Vai people, not my family.

Brewerville has a boarding school named after the African American Baptist minister and physician who was one of the founders of the colony of Liberia. Lott Carey School has a history of support by African Americans who financed Baptist missionary work in Africa without knowing much about Liberia.

My uncle, William Wilson, got married in Brewerville. He had just built his house about a street away from my grandmother's, which is across the street from the one I am building. Uncle William was a "ladies' man" who abused alcohol. On his wedding day, I was in the backseat of his car as he ran errands. He was involved in an automobile accident. Drunk before the ceremony, he hit a taxi. I sustained cuts on my left arm, which left lifelong scars. The wedding was delayed by a few hours.

Brewerville weddings were elaborate with a church ceremony and large reception. Even if the marriage did not last like Uncle William's marriage to Aunt Sophia, the family ties were not easily broken.

I grew up attending Geda Chapel African Methodist Episcopal Church. Unless I had permission from my mother, I had to be in church every week. Active in Sunday school, I was expected to give a recitation on Easter. At a Sunday school convention, I was recognized as a youth leader.

Church provided many opportunities. I practiced public speaking and learned that preachers were not saints. The presiding elder, the married head preacher of our district, had a sexual relationship with one of my relatives. The teenager had a child for him.

The churches in Brewerville provided a religious rite of passage for teenagers. One church hosted the annual weeklong revival. Families encouraged teenagers fourteen to sixteen-years-old to go to the mourners' bench where they knelt and prayed to "get religion." Getting religion involved being visited by the Holy Spirit, which included leaping, running, and shouting through the streets, "I got it! I got it!" This demonstration represented a self-centered adolescent emerging as a Christian adult.

My childhood included memorable experiences like listening to the radio, playing with my cousins, and fetching water and wood. Grandma's house was a safe haven for young and old and was always overcrowded with family, friends, and strangers. When I was about six years old, a fifteen-year-old friend of my aunt sought temporary shelter with us. As we lay in bed, she molested me. I told my Aunt Marie, and she confronted the molester. I rarely saw this "friend" after the incident. Sexual abuse of children was common in this community. I later learned that my molester had been molested by a well-known adult.

My first consensual sex occurred at sixteen years old in my grandmother's house. Older teen relatives were the primary sexual educators, which led to many unprepared teen parents.

Building families was difficult due to the lack of employment. Since Brewerville was not a farming or a fishing community, residents sought employment in Monrovia, or at iron ore mining companies.

My maternal grandfather, Isaac Roberts, worked for a mining company in Bomi Hills, now Tubmanburg, to sustain his family. He lost a leg in a railroad accident and had to retire. My stepfather, Charles Gibson, worked at a mining company in Yekepa, Nimba. He purchased equipment for the company. My mother worked at the Ministry of Education in Monrovia as a telephone operator. I visited her at work and watched her operate the switchboard. Due to their employment, my parents supported and educated eight children. Seven of us earned master's degrees and I, a doctorate degree.

With few businesses, the village had five churches and three schools. The schools produced many highly educated Brewervillans including Edwin J. Barclay, Liberia's eighteenth president. During the civil war, most of these institutions were destroyed.

My mother spent most of her life in Monrovia and lived in Brewerville during her final years. Like many elders of the family, she died in my grandmother's house.

Brewerville now has a mayor, city hall, bank, motel, and several businesses. It is a suburb of Monrovia with an influx of new residents and homes.

My grandmother, Mai Shaw had the most influence on me. She was more approachable than my mother. Her home was a sacred refuge for the birth, life, and death of scores of people. Her home provided me space to discover myself and my calling. My grandmother lived to be 89 years old.

She, her mother, Sarah Shaw; my mother, Elizabeth Flowers-Gibson; my stepfather, Charles Gibson Sr.; my brother, Dechonte; Uncle William Wilson, and Aunt Arona Marshall are buried in the cemetery, which is visible from my grandmother's backyard.

Boikai S. Twe

Chapter 6

Parenthood

"It takes a village to raise a child."
— African proverb

My grandmother had four daughters and three sons. My grandfather worked in Bomi Hills, while my mother and Uncle William were in Monrovia starting careers in government. My father was a member of the House of Representatives of Liberia and later Chairman of the Elections Commission.

My cousin, Berline, and I began kindergarten together. Our absent fathers required us to be raised by my grandmother and uncles. I moved to live with my mother at eight-years old.

My mother was single with two sons, Alex and me. She worked two jobs spanning from 8 a.m. to 11 p.m. Her work schedule left us unsupervised and free to roam the streets of Monrovia. My mother dated several men until she met Charles Gibson, Sr. Uncle William introduced them in 1960. A year later, they had a son, Harald, and got married soon after.

Charles Gibson, Sr. became my "Godpa" and provided immediate stability to the family. Godpa and my mother had three more sons, Charles, Albert (Dechonte), and Francis. They adopted two more children, Alfred and

Clayonon, Godpa's cousin and niece. I grew up in an immediate family of seven boys and one girl in Twe Farm, Bushrod Island.

Godpa and my mother were hard workers who put in long hours. The absence of my biological father affected my sense of identity. I often wondered why he was not involved in my life. In elementary school, I skipped school frequently walking the slums and beaches of Monrovia. As a grona boy, I searched for what I was missing.

On one occasion, a friend of my mother spotted me playing football on the beach at Coconut Plantation. She drove me to my mother's job. My mother took me to school and discovered that I had been absent for about two months. She had no idea because every day I dressed for school. She worked to pay for my tuition to a Catholic school and I frustrated her. She asked a neighbor to give me a whipping because she was tired of disciplining me and Godpa was away for training.

Mr. Chenoweth was the neighborhood disciplinarian. When he was around, children monitored their behaviors. My mother sought his help to make me aware of the seriousness of my offense and to feel the consequences of skipping school. With her permission, he gave me a whipping that left a lasting impression. This practice of neighbors helping parent children is common in Africa.

The nurturing and discipline I received from my family and community helped to move me back into the classroom with increased confidence and purpose. At Ricks, I was a member of the class called "Scorpions", the Class of 1971. The bonding that occurred as a result of living and going to school together fostered solidarity among classmates. We maintain contact and are supportive of each other.

I have served as a mentor to many at-risk youths, but

parenting posed some personal challenges. My parents supported eight children to obtain advanced degrees; however, I have had difficulty getting two of my three sons to complete college.

My second son is the product of my first romantic love with Cecelia Massaquoi. My absence from his life mirrored my childhood experience. Armah Thomas Massaquoi graduated from college with degrees in philosophy and sociology. He published a book of poetry and a memoir about his life and photography in Texas. These books reflect his struggle growing up and his determination to be successful.

Emman and Dakona, my sons with my wife, sought careers in the music industry. These Hip-Hop artists are students of the school of hard knocks, which is the best, but the hardest school. Dakona, my youngest son, is married with four non-biological children.

My sons were supported by an extended family and have grown up to be responsible, productive adults.

Chapter 7

Spirituality

"Everywhere there is sky, there is spirit."
— Mande proverb

Spirituality has been present among Africans since the birth of human beings on the continent. It existed for thousands of years before the Hebrews gave birth to Abrahamic faiths: Judaism, Christianity, and Islam. Africans of the diaspora separate spirituality from religion by focusing on internal goodness and a personal relationship with a higher power. Their religions are group expressions and practices of spirituality. Some have been forced to abandon African forms of spirituality and religion to adopt European and Arab forms. As a result, they have lost internal goodness and personal relationship with their higher power. White supremacy has hidden their self-knowledge and divinity.

In 1989, Daudi Azibo, a psychologist, linked this cultural domination to two psychological disorders:

1. Menticide — the destruction of the African mind. This term was first coined by Bobby E. Wright. It may explain the terrorism by Boko Haram, Al Shabaab, and the Lord Resistance Army who murder women and children to establish their religious extremism.

2. Misorientation—trying to live outside of an African belief system.

In articles, *A Review of African Psychology in West Africa* and *Crisis in West African Leadership*, I suggested that Africans must reclaim their sacred stories, institutions, and values. This change will lead them away from self-destruction toward a higher level of human life. To promote the reclamation of African spirituality, I assessed Christianity and Islam to show how they have been assimilated by some Africans, how they have been reconstructed to better fit African psychology, and how some Africans have created new forms of these religions to express their spirituality and psychology.

Impact of Christianity and Islam on African Psychology

Black psychologists, Na'im Akbar, Daudi Azibo, and I believe that adoption of foreign religions has introduced instability and inferiority into the African mind.

In 2015, Douglas E. Thomas wrote,

> "The human mind can function under severe pressure, but chaos is a formidable psychological weapon that causes the mind to shut down. The acceptance of one's cultural self brings mental clarity."[17]

The origins of Christianity and Islam in Judaism is worth examining to get clarity on their growing influence on African psychology.

---

[17] Thomas, Douglas E. *African Traditional Religion in the Modern World.* 2ed. McFarland, 2015.

I attended Yosef ben-Jochannan's lecture and read his book, *African Origins of the Major Western Religions*. He explained how African indigenous religions from Egypt provided the foundations for Judaism and the teachings of Moses. This view of Judaism and Moses was explained in Sigmund Freud's 1939 book, *Moses and Monotheism*. Sigmund Freud is considered one of the fathers of Western psychology and a great scholar of modern philosophy.

The concept of the creation of human beings by God (Ptah or Ra) originated in traditional African religion and philosophy. The concept of an almighty God and life after death existed in traditional African religion and philosophy thousands of years before Hebrews were in Egypt.

The first Hebrews were Africans who adopted the revolutionary concept of monotheism that emerged during the seventeen-year reign of Pharaoh Amenhotep IV in the middle of the 14th century B.C. Amenhotep was a devoted believer of one god: Aten, the sun god. Gary Greenberg, an American psychotherapist, explained that Amenhotep's one-god reform brought massive resentment throughout Egypt. Upon his death, his successor, Pharaoh Horemheb (King Tut), launched a campaign to restore the tradition of many lesser gods and erase all memory of Amenhotep. Loyal Amenhotep followers like Moses were banished from the country. These native Egyptians became outsiders in their own land. They rebelled and formed the House of Israel under the leadership of Moses. This story of Judaism gave birth to the Black Hebrew Israelites of Jamaica in the 1920s and Chicago in the 1960s.

The Black Power Movement of the 1960s brought the Black Hebrew Israelites to Monrovia. Self-determination motivated the Black Hebrew Israelites to move back to Africa and eventually to Israel in the 1970s. Hebrew theology gave birth to Christianity and Christian theology helped shape the theology of Islam.

Despite the one-god concept originating in African religion, Christianity and Islam have become cultural tools to promote White European and Arab male superiority. These religions contributed to the mental enslavement and death of millions of Africans in the name of bringing "civilization and peace."

In retrospect, stories of our exile and migration are popular themes in African religion/spirituality, "where the stone that was rejected by the builder has come to be the head cornerstone." (Psalm 118:22) The invaders of Africa used our reliance on spirituality and stories to divide, enslave, and exploit us. They claim we are superstitious and rely on witchcraft while they use books and science to exploit and keep us in inferiority.

This long history of deception, lies, and violence has left us in darkness, which some psychologists refer to as traumatic slavery syndrome. Our enslavers used the deadly science of violence and deception to maintain control over our minds. They used White Christianity and Islam to deceive and control us. Many of us have learned to distrust our culture and sciences in the face of deception and manipulation. We must reclaim our religion/spirituality and history to regain our humanity and divinity.

African spirituality and religion have been studied as a science by Christian scholars since the work of Edward Wilmot Blyden in the 19th century. Hence, most studies of African religio-cultural movements have been done from a Christian perspective. In the book, *African Religion in Western Scholarship*, Okot p'Bitek criticized African Christian scholars for trying to "dress up African deity in European garb." He accused Jomo Kenyatta, J.B. Danquah, K.A. Busia,

Mbiti and others of making African spirituality and religion conform to European beliefs and values.

I read the ideas of these Christian scholars and did not see their works as harmful to African spirituality. However, p'Bitek suggests that these Christian African scholars are promoting a theology of dominance which has inferiorized African people. They attack our African sacred stories that are the roots of Judaism, Christianity, and Islam and their African cultural identity.

I observed African Christians and Muslims at war with their African cultural rituals and identity. They worship European and Arab cultures and heroes while attacking African culture and sacred stories. Mental chaos and inferiority are evident among leaders, scholars, and youth all over Africa. This mental capture can be linked to our loss of wealth and power. Because of violence, poverty, and exploitation, we accept the lies of European and Arab missionaries. We are being misled by people who are confused about who they are and their purpose. This obsession with European and Arab religions has created inhumanity and destruction in Somalia, Democratic Republic of the Congo, Rwanda, Libya, and South Sudan, to name a few.

Some sought to reconstruct Christianity and Islam to better meet African cultural needs. Rastafari and the Nation of Islam are two examples in the African diaspora of this reconstruction of African religion/spirituality. These Black religio-cultural groups came out of Marcus Garvey's Back-to-Africa Pan-African movement. Their synthesis of African cultural rituals with Jewish, Christian, and Islamic doctrines have attracted millions of Africans.

Many use these spiritual hybrids to better understand and confront their oppression and enslavement. In the case of the Nation of Islam, they hosted the 1995 Million Man March, the largest peaceful demonstration of Black men in history. I attended this historical spiritual event which began with traditional African drumming and libation. More than one million Black men gathered in Washington, DC to atone and rededicate themselves to self-realization. This gathering reminded me of what Black Muslims teach: Black man is God. I left inspired and rejuvenated.

Rastafari, on the other hand, used reggae music and Ethiopianism to spread the message of Pan-Africanism and influence the consciousness of millions. When I traveled to India, London, Mexico, Canada, the Caribbean, and throughout Africa, I saw the impact that Rastafari and reggae music had on youth and elders. Bob Marley died more than thirty-seven years ago, but his songs have become spirituals of Pan-Africanism, equal rights, and justice for all.

Reggae artists sing of freedom and redemption. Rastafari has advocated for the medical use of marijuana since the 1940s. Today, marijuana is recognized as a medical wonder drug. Rastas helped revive African cultural unity and history. Rastas reason that man is God and God is "I n I", Black man and woman.[18] In Rastafari and the Nation of Islam, African cultural stories have been blended with Abrahamic beliefs to reach the captive Africans and the dispossessed of capitalism. This reconstructionist approach to African religion/spirituality pushes back the darkness of inferiority but does not free us to bathe in the African sun of self-knowledge and divinity. It provides sparks of light to truth, justice, and love in the world of moral darkness and death.

---

[18] Faristzaddi, Millard. *Itations of Jamaica and Rastafari*. Judah Anbese, 1987.

Psychology of African Religion

A systematic way of looking at religion is to understand how people tell stories about who they are, from where they came, and where they are going to express their spirituality. The stories provide a sense of purpose and a goal they want to achieve in life and death. Religion gives people power within their economy, education, government, military, culture, art and music, architecture, funerals/burials, and relationships. Our 500-year loss of "higher power" in these areas led to inferiorities in our culture.

I taught Traditional African Religion (TAR) in African American Studies and African psychology since 1990. I explained TAR as sacred stories or myths that we tell to describe our identity, purpose, and direction in life and the afterlife. Like Christianity and Islam, TAR emerged in a cultural context where we elevated African cultural values and rituals to be sacred. In TAR, we elevate ourselves and leaders to levels of divinity. I instruct students that African science, dance, drumming, dress, food, arts, and environment are sacred in TAR and can be used for self-elevation.

In contrast, our cultural arts and values are forbidden or marginalized in Islam and Christianity. Our concepts of God developed in Vodu (Voodoo), Abosom, Orisha, Chi, Imana, and Bwami are cultural stories and myths to maintain our identity and community. Hence, our spirituality is rooted in African cultural rituals, which Christianity and Islam attempt to degrade as devilish. I pour libation, an African ritual, for various public and family events. This act represents connection between past and present, physical, and spiritual, children and ancestors. The ritual demonstrates our intention for self-extension and divinity.

Some African Christians and Muslims are fearful of participating in libation. They offer a prayer to publicly declare their religious allegiance. They have replaced African spirituality with White-male spirituality and superiority.

A spiritual tradition that many of us practiced before colonialism is making sacrifices. Sacrifices are the primary means used to restore communal balance, relations with God, and ancestors. This TAR practice has assimilated into Christianity and Islam. A sacrifice is a petition to a higher power just like a prayer. Sacrifices can offer an animal or money. In the past, people were murdered to avert failure in business or politics or promote recovery from an illness.

In Africa, ritual murder is one of the worst crimes that one can commit. Boko Haram in West Africa, Al Shabaab in East Africa, and the Lord Resistance Army in Central Africa sacrifice innocent lives to prevent their political failures and extinction. They have reverted to barbarism and darkness to spread doctrines of inhumanity and war. In most parts of Africa, an animal or money is used as a substitute for the vital energy of a person. Without sacrifice, harmony cannot be restored in the face of chaos. Risk and sacrifice are required to bathe in the sunshine of freedom and self-determination.

Those who practice TAR are community oriented. With traditional African thought, individual freedom exists within a communal context. Rastafari uses the term "I n I" (we) to describe the individual and the collective. The African self is a spirit that is engaged in self-extension and self-realization. The sacrifices throughout Africa are means of maintaining community cohesion and wholeness. The opposite is obtained by Muslim and Christian extremists in Africa.

Worship in TAR involves rituals, rites of passage, and ceremonies that elevate our culture and ourselves to the status of sacred and cosmic consciousness. Our salvation is available through TAR and its melanin-dominant origins in Africa, not Rome, Jerusalem, or Mecca. The abandonment of our spirituality and cultural inventions has led to widespread corruption and inferiority complexes.

Traditional African religion does not seek converts to prove its validity. It is a way of life that is carried within our biogenetic makeup. Douglas E. Thomas wrote, "In traditional African communities one's family cult (culture) was also their 'religion'. Culture is religion".[19]

This idea was illustrated in my family. On her dying bed, my grandmother asked that no pastor preach her funeral. She wanted her family to be responsible for the funeral and eulogy. My brother, Alex, eulogized her.

Goals of African spirituality are self-mastery and pursuit of truth-justice. Those who attain these goals experience internal peace, happiness, and Zion. I sought these goals. Detachment from material possessions brought me closer to spiritual and cosmic consciousness. I follow a vegan diet and exercise in nature. Recognizing that spiritual progression is an individual and community effort, I encourage my family and community to do the same.

Suffering is a sign from the spiritual and mental worlds to look at our actions and thoughts more carefully. The balance of the forces of nature depends on human conduct. Suffering teaches us humility and sharing. Being rich in spirit is the true measure of wealth. My grandmother's house was a wooden shack; however, she was wealthy in

---

[19] Thomas, Douglas E. *African Traditional Religion in the Modern World.* 2ed. McFarland, 2015.

spirit. She used the available cultural and natural resources to live a divine life.

In TAR, God's self-disclosure or revelation is not static or recorded in a book like the Abrahamic religions. TAR is organic and open to new revelations unlike Christianity and Islam which have fixed doctrines and Scriptures. In African storytelling, we elevated Harriet Tubman, Ida B. Wells-Burnett, Edward W. Blyden, Marcus Garvey, W.E.B. Du Bois, Kwame Nkrumah, and Bob Marley to Pan-African prophets who introduced new revelations on African unity and spirituality. The African Union is concrete evidence of this understanding and Rastafari creates songs and stories of our spiritual reawakening. All over Africa and the diaspora, African youth and elders chant poems, sing songs and tell stories of unity and redemption. These messages are about African ancestors, sacrifices, and achievements. Steel Pulse, a reggae group from the U.K., sang lyrics in "Not King James Version" indicating that the Garden of Eden was in Africa and most of the biblical prophets were Black men.

A third approach to African religion/spirituality can be described as the constructionist response that contributes to critical self-knowledge and elevation in a world of darkness and White supremacy. This approach, mentioned on page 35, is a compilation of cultural rituals, practices, and values. Diverse and embracive of cultural forms and natural environments, it promotes our right relations with the world. It claims that the Creator or Vital Force (Ptah or Ra) placed helper spirits in charge of earthly affairs that created everything in existence, including human beings. Douglas E. Thomas wrote, "Since energy can neither be created nor destroyed. Traditional Africans view physical death as a transition from one form to another. Death is a gateway by which one enters the afterlife."[20]

Libation opens the gates of Zion. I used libation to honor ancestors because they advocated for me and other relatives. Libation creates and maintains our collective memory and sense of divinity. Our ancestors watch over family members and become our primary advocates and protectors. As a result, invoking ancestors in rituals like libation provides protection and self-extension.

From the constructionist perspective, our ancestors, cultural forms, values, stories, and songs offer protection and memories in this world and the next. Without this connection to collective memories, one can die a bad death and not become an ancestor. We are replacing sacred traditions and cultural resources with confusion and corruption. TAR brings balance and harmony.

Advances in African science are increasing our self-knowledge and self-extension. My study of cultural rituals, stories, songs, languages, and symbols contributed to my understanding of science and other systems of knowledge. I learned that African science and religion are complementary, not contradictory. These truths are studied and transferred in African secret societies.

African leaders like Nkrumah and Selassie saw science and cultural arts as indispensable to African unity and progress. African science and arts help shape the modern world through its diffusion and reconstruction in the African diaspora. Negro spirituals, jazz, blues, gospel, rock and roll, rhythm and blues, reggae, and hip-hop are indispensable cultural arts to human well-being and unity. African science has become a dominant force in the global

---

[20] Thomas, Douglas E. *African Traditional Religion in the Modern World*. 2ed. McFarland, 2015.

popular culture. Black African origins of philosophy, ethical values, writing, paper, mapmaking, navigation, textile chemistry, astronomy, medicine, and mathematics contribute to human advancement and elevation.

Chapter 8

Disorientation and Disorders

"If you keep the company of thieves, you will become one."
— Congolese proverb

From the birth of the Republic of Liberia, our leaders conspired with the American Colonization Society to destroy or discredit African culture and use capitalism and Christianity as pillars of the state. In the 1820s, leaders of the American Colonization Society saw themselves as civilized Christians and Africans as uncivilized pagans. This lie led to the disorientation of state power toward exclusion, violence, and injustice against indigenous Africans. The state attempted to operate as a "little" America/Babylon in Africa by duplicating the republican system of the U.S.A. This system centralized state power in the hands of a few settler families. The promotion of capitalism and private property by the state led to widespread private control of land and exploitation of the rural population.

Liberian leaders attempted to blame African culture for slavery and disorder in the region. African culture was attacked as uncivilized and demonic, while American culture and values were imposed as social standards. This imposition by state leaders led Liberians to have an unclear view of ourselves, society, and the world. Our leaders conspired with capitalists and criminals to worship money, status, violence, Christian and Muslim heroes, and to denigrate African heroes, resources, women, and youth.

My father wrote a poem about this travesty. In his poem, "The Tom-Toms Beat No More", he sent a clarion call about Africa's loss of vigilance and self-preservation. The warning drums that prepared us to resist and fight "dangerous foes" had gone silent. He questioned whether "pale-faced" strangers had charmed with glittering gifts "to still that passion for the land where our Father's bones are laid."[21]

His warning about loss of vigilance and connections to our land and culture is true today.

I experienced disorientation when I attended a Catholic elementary school in Monrovia. Surrounded by images of White Jesus and Mary, I was indoctrinated in catechism class. I told my mother that I wanted to become a Catholic.

In anger, she said, "You can become whatever you want after you grow up and leave my house."

I was surprised by her reply because I was trying to fit in with the Catholics. My family was African Methodist.

Daudi Azibo suggested that mental order is being in harmony with one's culture, God, and natural laws.[22] Disorders occur when one chooses to live outside the African values system. Disorders were observed in Brewerville, when returned Africans sought to recreate southern American culture, churches, and schools. The Poro and Sande Societies of the Gola and Vai people were seen as

---

[21] Thomas, H. Carey. "The Tom-Toms Beat No More." In A. Doris Banks Henries (Ed.) *Poems Of Liberia: 1836-1961.* (pp.84-85). Macmillan. 1963.

[22] Azibo, Daudi, A.Y. "Moving Forward with Legitimation of the Azibo Nosology II". *Journal of African American Studies,* 19 (3) (p.p.298-318) 2015.

demonic and uncivilized.

As youth, we were taught to fear this aspect of village life and embrace the stories that we were Americo-Liberians and ex-slaves of America or Babylonians. These lies and contradictions led to alcohol abuse and domestic violence. This anchoring of Liberian culture in American history and religion led to disorientation and disorders in Liberian psychology. African literature helped me reject the lies of White superiority to see African culture from a Pan-African perspective. These lies continue to be promoted by churches, mosques, schools, universities, non-governmental organizations (NGOs), United Nations, and media.

In *The Wretched of the Earth*, Fantz Fanon suggested that the path to self-destruction begins with self-doubt, denial, self-mutilation, and suicide. Self-doubt led to the underdevelopment of African culture, resources and products, and the importation of American, European, Chinese, and Arab cultures and products. Denial has caused Liberians to claim they were never colonized or enslaved, and that African people are uncivilized. Self-mutilation led to ethnic divisions and the exploitation of women and youth for personal wealth and power. Years of civil disorder in Liberia led to widespread exploitation, neglect, and abuse of children.

In 1979, youth leaders educated in the U.S. challenged the corruption of Liberian leaders, which led to the 1979 Rice Riot. Hundreds of citizens were hurt or killed. I returned to Liberia and observed the despair of the youth. I warned friends that the riotous violence unleashed was due to frustration of the youth and grona boys about their oppression by the "big people" in Monrovia.

In his writing, Fanon explained, "When we [youth] revolt, it's not for a particular culture. We revolt simply because, for many reasons, we no longer breathe."[23]

One year later, Samuel Kanyon Doe and twelve semi-literate, young soldiers trained by the U.S. staged a coup. They ended the almost 100-year rule of the True Whig Party. President William R. Tolbert was murdered, and several government officials were executed. Youth and indigenous Liberians took a breath of freedom. My father was arrested and jailed as a government official. He died in jail without access to medication for his diabetes.

The People Redemption Council that assumed control of the government declared that they had come to bring an "end to corruption." The new military government was supported by U.S. President Ronald Reagan and the government of Israel. The new government held elections and Samuel K. Doe, although too young to run based on the constitution, was elected president. Oppression by the "Congoes" of Monrovia was replaced by the oppression of the Krahn, President Doe's ethnic group. To maintain power, President Doe arrested and executed his opponents and other ethnic groups, especially the people of Nimba County. Liberians lost our freedom and headed for self-destruction and suicide.

In 1989, Charles Taylor, who escaped from prison in the U.S., invaded Liberia with a small group of fighters recruited from Nimba County. This action led to more than fourteen years of civil crisis, 250,000 deaths, and destruction of the state. Children, ten-to-thirteen years old, were put on the frontline as soldiers. I traveled to Monrovia during the first year of the civil crisis, to rescue my mother. She suffered a stroke in Roycesville, an area controlled by Charles Taylor and his forces. Travelling into this environment of death and

---

[23] Fanon, Fantz. *Black Skin, White Masks*. Grove Press. 1952.

destruction traumatized me. This war increased social and mental disorders and forced Liberians to migrate to other West African states. As refugees and displaced people, Liberians experienced the hospitality and support of West Africans and non-governmental organizations (NGOs).

On my way to Monrovia, I traveled through Freetown, Sierra Leone, and Abidjan, Ivory Coast. I witnessed the generosity of West Africans toward Liberian refugees. We learned to accept our African identity in West Africa.

In 1994, I spoke on this topic during a lecture at the University of Liberia. I suggested that Liberia would only see an end to war if we reconciled with our African identity and rejected the lie that we were a "little" Black America. I insisted that Liberian women needed to take leadership in government and the peace process to counterbalance the male warlords.

In the U.S., we organized to help bring an end to the civil crisis. I worked with a group to create the All Liberian Conference of North America. As a civic organization, we worked to contribute to the peace process and elections. We had four conventions: Atlanta, Georgia (1994), Cleveland, Ohio (1995), San Francisco, California (1996), and Arlington, Texas (1997).

Youth in the streets of Monrovia chanted during the presidential campaign of Charles Taylor, "You kill my Ma. You kill my Pa, but I'll vote for you!" President Charles Taylor increased the suffering of Liberia and its youth by his greed and violence. Liberians engaged in self-mutilation and suicide. He expanded his rule of terror and disorder into Sierra Leone and Guinea. In 2003, President Taylor was forced to leave Liberia by advancing armed groups and pressure from President George W. Bush. Liberia stepped back into the community of nations in 2005, when Ellen

Johnson Sirleaf, was elected president.

The post-traumatic stress disorder (PTSD) resulting from years of death and destruction has yet to be addressed through African rituals and healing. In 2007, I conducted workshops for mental health counselors at a college in Monrovia and healthcare providers at the Redemption Hospital in New Kru Town. I provided self-regulation and cognitive-behavioral techniques to help those with trauma. More mental health services are needed for youth who were the perpetrators and victims of violence. Many of them have become "zogos," dying slowly from neglect and trauma in the slums and forests of Liberia.

Chapter 9

The Art and Science of Healing

"Good health does not spread, disease does."
—Zulu proverb

The need for healing is evident given the more than 500 years of fighting enslavement and capitalist exploitation. Enslavement led to higher rates of heart disease, high blood pressure, obesity, diabetes, and cancer in Africans than in Europeans and Asians. Brutality and battles for self-determination introduced PTSD and traumatic slavery syndrome (TSS). Centuries of manipulation by Arab and European colonizers have led to increased rates of preventable medical problems and psychological disorders. Some researchers have shown that when we have one common preventable medical problem, we are more likely to report feeling depressed.[24] Failure to acknowledge our experiences of assaults and manipulations leads to the spread of diseases and disorders.

Years of wars in Liberia illustrated the need to speak out

---

[24] Trivedi, Madhukar H. "The Link between Depression and Physical Symptoms." *Primary Care Companion to The Journal of Clinical Psychiatry.* 2004, 6 (supplement 1): 12-16.

against proxy wars and robbery of our resources. A casual observation of the physical, psychological, and spiritual destruction suggests needs for peace, health, and healing. We need Pan-Africanism to help drive out 500 years of pain and suffering.

My desire to become a healer came as I observed and participated in the disorders that surrounded my childhood. Ma Mai used herbs, utterances, practices, and natural objects to heal our illnesses as children. She used her relationships within the community, church, and Ma Sando, who lived across the street, to prevent and intervene in disorders and diseases. I remember her using fever tea, lemongrass, life-everlasting leaf, and alligator pepper to treat illnesses. She was unable to heal Aunt Nora, her daughter, an alcoholic who physically abused some of the children at home. Ma Mai warned, "Nora! Don't hurt da child." This admonishment only postponed the inevitable abuse.

Healing is an ancient practice which goes back to the beginning of humanity. This practice was—and is—mostly psychosomatic involving mind and body. In our healing traditions, the practitioner uses the power of words along with the potency of rituals, talismans, herbs, and roots to treat diseases. In ancient Egypt, healers interpreted dreams to treat some illnesses and disorders. The use of plant oils for treating diseases, known today as aromatherapy, originated in Africa. Magical perfumes in ancient Africa were used to increase one's intuition, foresight, and inner vision. Evidence shows that ancient Egyptians used yoga and hypnotherapy in their healing practices. The development of extraordinary mental concentration and self-mastery were techniques also used. The ability to reestablish contacts with healthy life-giving forces within oneself and the community is crucial to healing.

Today, in most parts of Africa, illness is an expression of drama, which is physical and spiritual. Human beings have earthly and spiritual lives, which involve their past and future. The nature of healing is an art and science in Africa.

In his novel, *The Healers*, Ayi Kwei Armah suggested that the African "healer must first have a healer's nature," which he defined as the "capacity for constant inspiration." This quality reflects the artistic nature of healing. The healer requires training and preparation which points to the science involved. The healer stands on the side of truth, harmony, and justice and against manipulation and disorder. The morality of the healer is crucial for the success of the treatment.

Using Armah's perspective inspired me to write "The Black Spark" as a symbol of my Black consciousness and recovery. A year later, I was called to be a psychologist/healer. I began my career as a healer with the Urban Youth Council. Without training, I used inspiration from African literature to counsel and assist youth with their personal growth and struggle against poverty. I offered support and services that I watched my grandmother give.

As my formal education and career ensued, the work at Longview State Hospital became uninspiring. I pondered about how I could use African psychology in U.S. clinical settings. I wrestled with this matter until I returned to Monrovia in 1979 to visit my stepfather who had had a stroke. I observed the youth of Monrovia being hungry for a change after the 1979 Rice Riot. I realized I needed to prepare myself to serve at-risk youth victimized by greed and abuse.

While at UC, I helped to establish the Rastafari community of Cincinnati. I met and reasoned with other Rastas about community development. I grew my hair in dreadlocks, a sign of my return to a natural African "livity" or lifestyle. I also studied and affiliated with the All-African People's Revolutionary Party (AAPRP). This socialist political party was founded by Kwame Nkrumah and organized in Conakry, Guinea in 1968 by Stokley Charmichael (Kwame Ture). These two Pan-African organizations assisted with my training and preparation in African psychology. Rastafari provided a cultural and spiritual foundation and AAPRP provided a political Pan-African direction.

In 1990, I became the educational consultant for the emerging W.E.B. Du Bois Academy. This Afrocentric elementary school created drugs and violence prevention curricula to complement the Dayton Public Schools' curriculum. I trained teachers and provided workshops for the students. My training and preparation as a healer became more specialized when I trained in the Simba Na Malaika Wachanga (Afrocentric Rites of Passage) Organization in 1992. Some members of our jamaa (family) trained to become medical doctors, nurses, and social workers. This training made me look inward to prepare youth and adults to be warriors, nation builders, and healers.

I collaborated with BarbaraO; Mama O as some of us called her. She was an actor and healer who created a documentary on African and other indigenous healers. She introduced me and some of my students to the techniques and practices she learned on her journey into the art and science of traditional healing. We worked together to host an African World Films Festival in 2008 and 2009.

Since 1992, I trained hundreds of students in African-centered education and African psychology. I helped build and maintain Pan-African organizations and institutions while looking for ways to heal the traumas of enslavement and mental disorders.

Boikai S. Twe

Chapter 10

Community Psychology

"It is a propitious omen for the future that at this very moment, the free nations of Africa are giving tangible evidence of their determination to work together not only for their own good, but for the good of Africa and the entire world."
—Emperor Haile Selassie I, 1958

African community psychology has produced a revolution in community empowerment which is leading to a revolution in human development. The African Liberation Movement of the 1950s and 1960s led to social and political actions that brought an end to colonial rule in Africa and the end to legalized racial segregation in the U.S.

The origins of community psychology in the U.S. can be traced to the research and advocacy of Kenneth and Mamie Clark, a husband-and-wife team of psychologists. They designed and conducted a series of experiments known as "the doll tests" to study the psychological effects of racial segregation on African American children during the 1940s. They found a majority of the children preferred the white doll and assigned positive characteristics to it. The black doll was seen as "bad", "ugly," and "dumb." This research and their conclusions influenced The U.S. Supreme Court's 1954 decision in the Brown v. Board case to desegregate American public education. This brought an end to legalized racial segregation and the advancement of civil rights for Africans in the U.S. and the world.

The founding of the Organization of African Unity and Association of Black Psychologists is evident of this era of revolution. This change in Pan-African consciousness contributed to a change in science, psychology, and the introduction of Black Studies. Community psychology emerged as an area of specialization during this revolution.

My practice and teaching of community psychology used social and political actions to promote community change and wellness. I worked with other Liberians to create the Dayton Area Liberian Association and the All Liberian Conference to promote peace and end the Liberian Civil War. I led the creation of the Dayton Youth Violence Prevention Task Force which met for two years at the City Hall of Dayton. This taskforce was created to promote the prevention of youth violence in Dayton.

African community psychology has contributed to resource and capacity development in African communities. The development of the Economic Community of West African States (ECOWAS) and other regional economic communities of the African Union has moved us toward economic cooperation and self-determination. We have regional economic development plans for our resources and infrastructure.

In Dayton, I taught community psychology to improve community resources and capacity development. In 2016, Northwest Dayton, my neighborhood, organized to create a co-op called GEM City Market. This project was an attempt to address the issue of a food desert where fresh food markets and groceries were absent. The Dayton Africana

Elders Council agreed to support this effort led by Amaha Sellassie and Mama Nozipo Glenn. Community members were recruited to purchase ownership of the co-op, which operates to reduce hunger and obesity.

From 1990 to 2019, I worked with groups of youth and adults to develop Dayton's African community. We helped to develop the Dayton Rites of Passage, African American Culture Club, W.E.B Du Bois Academy, Dayton Mentorship Program, ABLE Youth Leadership Institute, and Dayton Africana Elders Council. These organizations and projects used African and African American literature, holidays, languages, and cultural arts to racially socialize members of our community.

Some of us tend to overemphasize European or Arab heritage and culture over our own.

Students often asked, "How do we develop ourselves and our African community?"

This question has been investigated by scientists and scholars of the 21st century. I tried to answer this question through my practice and teaching of psychology. In 1992, Kobi K.K. Kambon attempted to answer this question when he wrote, "Virtually every basic feature of the African people's unique/distinct lifestyle can be argued to flow through the African Self-Extension Orientation/African Self-Consciousness core of African personality."[25] This description of our personhood and community goes beyond place of birth or skin color. It focuses on the character, self-knowledge, oneness-harmony with nature, communalism, group survival, Africentric values, beliefs, attitudes, and behaviors.

---

[25] Kambon, Kobi K.K. *The African Personality in America*. Nubian Nation. 1992.

The research of Cheikh Anta Diop, Kobi Kazembe Kalongi Kambon and other Pan-African scientists can be used to educate and construct healthy communities. Being educated requires understanding scientific evidence that Africa is the birthplace of humans and acknowledging that only one human race exists, not many different races.

The ongoing political and economic cooperation in Africa, especially in West Africa, is improving our movement across ethnic and national boundaries. African economic cooperation is leading to increased regional understanding and unity. The African Union is working to reduce religious extremism and colonial divisions. We must confront the ongoing traumas of enslavement and colonization to emancipate ourselves from mental and economic slavery. We must no longer promote Arab and European cultures and languages over our own.

Within the Economic Community of West African States (ECOWAS), we traveled under one passport and adopted the eco as our common currency. These practices advance our self-extension and self-consciousness. ECOWAS is creating a communal psychology that will make political and economic unity a reality to marginalized and rural Africans.

Educational systems need to promote our culture, science, languages, and literature. African community psychology can free us from self-doubt and incompetence. African science, technology and art can be applied to promote political and economic development that will reduce psychological and physical migration.

We can develop communities by using new cultural tools like SMART AFRICA, which uses information and communication to revolutionize agriculture, education, health, housing, transportation, and governance. My experience has shown me that African community psychology is global. It transcends race and place of birth. Digital technology and the smartphone are making information and communities more accessible and global. I maintain ties to Liberia and the U.S. through the internet and smartphone.

In 1986, Wade Nobles suggested that African community psychology rests on reclaiming the African ancestry of humanity. It represents the systematic summation of ideas, beliefs, and knowledge of African people being applied for human development and liberation. More attention is being paid to Africa and its growing role in the economic, political, industrial, and spiritual development of the world.

If you study European and Arab movements, they show trends of destabilization and destruction of people and their cultures, which raises questions about their intentions and use of religion for wealth-seeking. These cultures and religions are used to justify terrorizing and enslaving us. These international terrorists must be seen as creators of chaos and injustice. They spread terror and war, and in some cases, genocide.

This issue was taken up by the United Nations World Conference against Racism, Racial Discrimination, Xenophobia and Related Intolerance in Durban, South Africa in 2001. Dayton was represented by Dean Lovelace and Vernella Randell, outstanding African Americans who fought against racism. The African diaspora arrived at this conference seeking justice for the crimes of slavery, colonization, and genocide. They were betrayed by African heads of state who sided with the U.S., European Union, and Israel, and rejected the demand for reparation and justice. This betrayal demonstrated that African state leaders cannot be trusted to fight for truth-justice. The African diaspora must provide leadership on this issue like it did for Pan-Africanism.

African philosophy and psychology have reemerged as essential parts of the global popular culture and liberation struggle. African community psychology speaks to the human spirit in ways that mainstream religions, languages, and art cannot. This ongoing challenge to European and Arab cultural domination represents the reascension of African community development in the modern world.

Chapter 11

Rastafari Community

"Where there is no vision, the people perish."
—Proverbs 29:18

My first month in the U.S. I met Ras Yakub, a Rasta. He lived near the University of Cincinnati campus and was a friend of TJ, a childhood friend from Monrovia. Ras Yakub was an African American who claimed an Ethiopian identity. He made a lasting impression on me with his knowledge and photos from Ethiopia.

He told me about the time he met an African American female at a bar.

He asked, "What's your name?"

"Shequana."

"That's not your real name. Your real name is Zauditu, Empress of Ethiopia." Yakub was a Rasta who viewed Ethiopia as Zion during the Black Power era. He wanted African Americans to shift their consciousness toward Africa, as many did not know their African roots. I was often impressed by his passion and commitment.

During the Black Power Movement, African names, music, and attire were popular. Cymande was a musical group of Rastas that played a fusion of jazz, funk, and reggae. I had purchased one of their albums while in Monrovia. The track, "Rastafarian Folk Song", was an A cappella chant.

In 1974, Bob Marley and the Wailers introduced the world to Rastafari through reggae music. Rastafari is a Jamaican "reconstructionist" socio-religious movement inspired by Marcus Garvey's Back-to-Africa project and the coronation of Ras Tafari and Wayzero Menan as Emperor Haile Selassie I and Empress Menan Asfaw of Ethiopia on November 2, 1930. The lyrics drew me into the songs, but it took me a while to dance to the rhythms. In "Africa Unite", Bob Marley sang that unification of Africans would benefit God and humanity because we are all children of Africa.

After graduating from Berea, I moved to Cincinnati looking for work and a community to sustain me when I first heard the Wailers' *Catch a Fire* and *Burnin'* albums. In 1978, I experienced Bob Marley and the Wailers in concert at Cobo Hall in Detroit. Following my second memorable encounter with Rastafari and its message, I read everything I could find on the subject.

My doctorate work brought me closer to Rastafari. I met students and youth who had an interest in reggae and Rastafari. We took a trip to Chicago in 1983 to celebrate Emperor Haile Selassie I's Earth Day (birthday) on July 23. This led us to hosting Rastafari celebrations at UC. At our first event, I read parts of the speech made by Emperor Haile Selassie I at the first Organization of African Unity (OAU) Summit in 1963.

He said:

> "Today, we look to the future calmly, confidently and courageously. We look to the vision of an Africa not merely free but united. In facing this new challenge, we can take comfort and encouragement from the lessons

of the past. We know that there are differences among us. Africans enjoy different cultures, distinctive values, special attributes. But we also know that unity can be and has been attained among men of the most disparate origins, that differences of race, of religion, of culture, of tradition, are no insuperable obstacle to the coming together of peoples. History teaches us that unity is strength and cautions us to submerge and overcome our differences in the quest for common goals, to strive, with all our combined strength, for the path to true African brotherhood and unity."[26]

My interest in reggae music led me to host Reggae Night at a neighborhood bar. I partnered with Ras Yahmin, a UC student. This project led other Rastas to host weekly reggae dance halls. When the Association of Black Psychologists held their International Convention in Cincinnati in 1984, they held a session on Rastafari to which we, Cincinnati Rastas, were invited.

My dissertation on African students' college and university experience in the United States was inspired by an interview with Emperor Haile Selassie I. Italian journalist, Oriana Fallaci, published it on June 24, 1973, in the *Chicago Tribune*. By 1986, Rastafari in Cincinnati had moved from a small group of friends to a thriving community of 150-200 members and their children. The community established two annual celebrations: Earth Day,

---

[26] *BlackPast*. "(1963) Haile Selassie, 'Toward African Unity'." 25 Sept. 2019, https://www.blackpast.org/global-african-history/speech-global-african history/1963-haile-selassie-towards-african-unity

which was Selassie's birthday (July 23) and Coronation Day, which was Selassie and Menan's coronation as emperor and empress (November 2).

During these celebrations, the community engaged in Nyabinghi drumming, workshops, and worship. Rastas, their family, and friends gathered to plot the road to Zion. At most of these celebrations, I spoke or conducted workshops. The most memorable "itations" (presentations) were a photo exhibit of trips to Accra, Ghana and Addis Ababa, Ethiopia; a proposal for a Rastafari Elders Council; the creation of a rites of passage program for the youth; and the year 2063 Agenda of the African Union.

In the presentation of my 2007 trip to Ghana, the country celebrated its 50th anniversary of independence. I showed photos of my visits to Kwame Nkrumah's Memorial Park, Cape Coast Slave Castles, and the Institute of Ethiopian Studies located at the University of Addis Ababa. The Institute preserved the living quarters of Emperor Haile Selassie I and Empress Menan, which confirmed to me that African psychology and spirituality are based on reason and verification.

My attempt to establish a Rastafari Elders Council took root but has been slow to develop. The rites of passage program was initiated but not sustained due to the lack of parental involvement.

Rastas in Cincinnati have reconstructed themselves from Black Hebrew Israelites and Black Nationalists to Rastafari and Ethiopian. Rasta women elevated Empress Menan as Omega. She is celebrated as the divine partner to Alpha, her husband, Selassie I. This recognition created a needed balance in male/female relationships in the male-dominated Rasta community.

Most of the world's renowned reggae bands have

performed in Cincinnati. They brought the message of Black liberation and African Unity to the 'Nati. In 2014, I worked with Ras Yahmin to bring Mutabaruka, the Jamaican poet and reggae artist, to The Black Man's Think at Sinclair College. Rastas from Cincinnati and Columbus attended. As the keynote speaker at this free, public event, Muta spoke about the importance of African liberation and unity. He brought a Rasta view to the Black Man's Think Tank that many Christian men did not appreciate because they perceived his message as critical of their religious beliefs. I hosted a reception for Muta at my home which was supported and attended by the community.

On my return to Monrovia in March 2019, I saw Rastas on the streets. I asked if the Rastafari had an organization and learned that Rastas had a roots/culture shop on South Beach. I visited Imperial Castle and found Jah Sammit making and selling arts and crafts on the beach.

The Imperial Castle, headed by Joseph Gardea, formed a partnership with the Monrovia branch of the Universal Negro Improvement Association (UNIA), Garvey's organization, to do a farm project. Joseph told me that Imperial Castle was working to establish a Pan-African Institute to re-educate and provide skills training for youth.

I discovered another Rasta organization: One Rastafari Foundation, the parent organization of Imperial Castle. Monrovian Rastas organized to improve their economic and social status and better contribute to Africa's development and redemption. The Rastafari Community of Monrovia, consisting of Imperial Castle and One Rastafari Foundation, gathered November 2 and 3, 2019 at Hotel Africa to celebrate Coronation Day and my Earth day (birthday). This show of "inity" (unity) also recognized that Rastafari "livity" is fullness (completeness). Rastas do not beg or seek aid from

Babylon. Rastafari reconstructs African lives. Reggae provides the soundtrack of our movement toward mental and economic emancipation.

Chapter 12

Ujamaa: Cooperative Economics

"If you only sleep, you will be hungry. If you only pray to God, you will be hungry. You will have to put in hard work."
– African proverb

In 1962, Julius Nyerere of Tanzania asserted that capitalism was brought into Africa by colonialism. For him, ujamaa reflected the African way of economic cooperation and equity. Nyerere, a Pan-Africanist and the first president of Tanzania, used ujamaa to appeal to our memory of sharing before the colonial era.

I became aware of the link between power, wealth, politics, and economics while studying with the All-African People's Revolutionary Party. However, this link was not clearly understood until I taught Africana Studies. I learned that wealth leads to power, which leads back to wealth. Those without wealth are controlled by the wealthy and powerful. This circular system represents the class struggle occurring in Africa and the diaspora. African politicians and wealthy elites strive to control and exploit the masses of marginalized, unemployed, and rural poor. For this reason, many want to become president, representatives, and senators.

Most people in my hometown worked low-paying jobs or cultivated a small farm or garden. These working-class families owned land and shared resources to meet needs. In contrast, Monrovia had obvious social class differences. The rich owned most of the land and had financial and social connections to pay for goods and services. The poor working class rented— some lived in slums like Westpoint—had little money, and minimal social services. Most of the rich had government jobs and political positions. The poor survived by selling in markets and working low-wage domestic and service jobs.

At St. Patrick Elementary School, students with rich parents rode to school in cars and had lunch money. Most of us walked to school with little lunch money. We put our money together to buy a loaf of bread and a can of sardines.

The need for money to survive became obvious when I was ten years old. My mother worked two jobs and tried to generate additional income with various projects. She baked corn bread and sold it at work. She invested about $25 US dollars to create a wooden vendor tray to sell cigarettes, candies, and gum. Peter, my foster brother, was responsible for selling at the movie theaters and bars in central Monrovia. On weekends and school breaks, I took Peter's place as a street vendor.

Being a street vendor taught me the value of money and how hard you have to work to keep from going under or to move up. I met TJ and Christopher Nippy, who were also selling on the streets. Better than I, they made more money. Christopher Nippy became a well-known football player and later worked at the Liberian Embassy in Washington, DC. TJ became president of Student Government of Tubman

High School and studied with me at Berea College.

At Ricks Institute, I earned spending money on Saturdays by cutting grass with a slasher, a tool similar to a sickle with a sharp metal blade. I worked up to five hours, callusing my hands, to earn one US dollar. We pooled our money for rice and corned beef. Someone volunteered their bucket to be used as the pot. At nightfall, we searched for a place to create a fire and secretly cook the rice. Whether we missed meals at the cafeteria, or didn't want to eat what was served, cooking became a cooperative project.

During school breaks, I worked in warehouses or repair shops as a clerk or technician. After high school, I volunteered with the Urban Youth Council. I earned a stipend, which came from fundraising and donations, as the coordinator of vocational guidance and counseling. Raising money taught me that people love the benefits of non-profit organizations, but do not donate money to them. To address the needs of the most vulnerable, one has to find ways to build cooperatives and obtain grants.

Attending Berea College showed me the dignity of labor and cooperative economics. Most students at Berea came from working class or poor households. We worked on campus to offset tuition and maintain the services of the college. This cooperative economics made Berea College one of the most endowed, small private colleges in the U.S. This tradition of elevating working class and poor students to achieve a college education made Berea College a highly-rated institution.

I worked at Duro Paper Bag Company in Covington, KY the summer following my freshman year. The job required me to lift 25-pound bales of paper bags every 30 seconds. The eight-hour shifts were grueling, the hardest job I had ever done. TJ and I pooled our money to buy a car. I learned to drive and got my driver's license in Kentucky. TJ eventually took ownership of the car and assisted me to buy my own, an Oldsmobile Delta 88. To earn gas money, I gave students rides for summer vacation and found a job in Providence, RI.

After college, it was hard to find a job, so I went back to Duro and began graduate studies at Xavier University in Cincinnati. I worked at Duro until I began my internship at Longview State Hospital. The monthly salary helped pay bills at the two-bedroom apartment I shared with a friend from Liberia, William Johnson.

In Cincinnati's Rasta community, businesses were created through cooperative economics. Records, books, and crafts were sold in Rasta shops, which promoted reggae dance halls and sold marijuana rolling papers and pipes. Marijuana was a major product for trade and access to cash. Others opened health food stores. Rastas, like Yahmin and David, spent several years in Federal prisons for trafficking marijuana. Others like Ras Machiel were murdered in robberies. Pooling labor and wealth can create businesses, reduce criminal activities, and eradicate poverty. Most Rastas in Cincinnati and Dayton avoided criminal activities through cooperatives and self-employment.

During a visit to Imperial Castle, I needed to urinate.

Jah Sammit said, "Go behind the building and piss against the wall."

Later, he suggested that I help them build a toilet. I contributed $500 to improve sanitation at the Castle and for the Rastafari community.

During the Liberian Civil War, we provided food and clothing to friends and relatives affected by the war. One project we supported was Bucket of Love started by Rev. Edward Peagler. Five-gallon plastic buckets filled with food and clothing were shipped to Monrovia for distribution. We raised money for this project by soliciting churches for donations. More than 1,000 buckets were shipped to Monrovia from 1995-1998.

Pooling money to complete a project or start a business is a common strategy used in Africa and the diaspora. In Liberia, it is called "joining susu." Susu allows a person to claim the pooled savings and contribute to the savings until every person in the group has been paid. People without bank accounts can save money and purchase high-cost items.

Cooperative economics makes business possible and profitable as evidenced by the growth in businesses owned and operated by the Fula people of Liberia. They combined their resources to become the fastest-growing African businesses in Liberia. The lack of capital or unwillingness to cooperate often leads to poverty, lack of social services, and criminal activities. Many people have gotten used to handouts and begging for bread like zogos (traumatized youth). We want to eat without cultivating food. We must relearn that dignity is in labor and avoid elites who live off bribes and political connections.

Chapter 13

Africana Studies

> "Africa is the origin of writing and the intellectual vocation."
> — African scholars

Teaching research methods and statistics at Denison University and Sinclair Community College helped me better understand the science of psychology. Testing hypotheses and conducting laboratory experiments with students taught me the importance of precision in science and the need for measurements. I made this area of psychology meaningful by connecting it to African liberation and the struggle for self-knowledge. Through Cheik A. Diop's writings, I discovered that scientific methods can be used to rediscover Africa's contributions to modern science.

Modern science now supports the Out of Africa theory of the origins of humans. Science supports that Kemet (Egypt), the greatest of African civilizations, was built by Black Africans from East and Central Africa. Modern science got writing and paper, geometry, engineering, medical textbooks, navigation, mapmaking, philosophy, and measurements from ancient Africa. This view of science made my understanding of research and statistics indispensable.

African understanding of the sun and its contributions to life was recorded in the *Hymn of Aton* around 1372 BC, before the rest of the world knew how to write. The *Hymn of Aton* states that the sun creates life and praises the star for embracing lands and all creations even in the depths of the sea. The poem attributes woman's ability to germinate seed and man's creation of semen to the sun.[27]

I trained in African American rites of passage, which had been developed by Maulana Karenga. The Simba Na Malaika Wachanga Organization (The Young Lions and Angels) of Dayton introduced me to the social theory of Kawaida and Black Cultural Nationalism. These ideas and practices grew out of the Black working class and poor people's struggle for equal opportunities and justice.

In 1991, an Ohio movement attempted to reduce the imprisonment and death of African American males. The University of Cincinnati hosted an annual Black Men's Think Tank that promoted Black consciousness. Afrocentrism emerged in the early 1990s from the work of Molefi Asante, influencing educational and mental health programs.

In 1992, African American students at Sinclair Community College asked for more Black Studies courses. They organized a student club, Because Our Time Is Now (BOTIN), and asked me to be the faculty adviser. This group facilitated a forum to discuss the state of Black students' educations. This forum recommended that a Black Studies program be created to support student success.

In 1995, I organized and hosted the annual Liberian Studies Association (LSA) Conference and became its

---

[27] "Aton Hymn". *Encyclopedia Britannica*, Encyclopedia Britannica, Inc., https://www.britannica.com/topic/Aton-Hymn.

president. This conference allowed local and international scholars to present papers on Liberia and West Africa. Scholars from the U.S., Liberia, Nigeria, Sierra Leone, and Israel attended this historic conference during the ongoing Liberian civil crisis.

I presented papers on Liberia and West Africa at LSA conferences from 1988-2009. Some papers presented were about African world views, African psychology, African extended family, Liberian disorders, Pan-Africanism, Edward W. Blyden, African Healing Practices, African Knowledge Systems, Economic Community of West Africa, and the All Liberian Conferences.

In 1999, I was invited as a guest lecturer at the School of Professional Psychology at Wright State University. I taught cross-cultural counseling techniques to doctoral students. I offered graduate students the opportunity to take Black Psychology as an independent study. Four doctorate students studied with me, and I was on the dissertation committees of two of them. In 2000, we offered three levels of Swahili as a part of the African American Studies curriculum. We added Rastafari and Reggae as a course in 2008.

In 2012, Sinclair College changed from quarters to semesters as part of a statewide mandate. This modification led to a change of African American Studies from a program to a short-term technical certificate.

Students, asked, "What can I do with a short-term technical certificate in African American Studies?"

"It can supplement your education in social work, law, teaching, and the growing STEM (Science, Technology, Engineering, and Math) fields."

Students earned this certificate by completing five courses: African American Studies, African American

Psychology, Survey of African History, African American History, and African American Literature.

Africana Studies at Sinclair contributed to the celebration of Kwanzaa in Downtown Dayton for more than thirty years. We created a Youth Harambee (Children Festival) for children four to twelve years old. For Black History Month, we created the Kuumba (Creativity) Celebration to provide students with opportunities for creative expressions and a talent showcase. We celebrated Black Love Day in February 2015. These four events were planned and hosted by students doing service learning in Africana Studies.

In 2016, I offered Africana Studies courses to high school students. Students at Thurgood Marshall High School earned college credits and increased their confidence. This outreach expanded to the Dayton College Preparatory Academy in 2017. Africana Studies contributed to increasing African American students' enrollment and completion of college. As reported in *Dayton Daily News,* African American students' graduation rate from 2013 to 2018 increased by more than 100%.

Chapter 14

Dayton Rites of Passage and ABLE Youth Leadership Institute

"The sun cannot be hidden."
— African proverb

In 1988, I was hired as an associate professor at Sinclair Community College. I infused Pan-African ideas and values throughout my instruction of general psychology. In the History of Psychology course, students learned that philosophy and medicine combined to form modern psychology.

I asked, "Who were the originators of philosophy and medicine?"

In scattered response, students said, "The Greeks, Socrates, and Hippocrates."

"Where did the Greeks get their philosophy and medicine? Were they the first ancient people to develop philosophy and medicine?"

One student said, "From the gods."

I explained that the Egyptians—Ancient Black Africans—were the "gods" who began writing philosophy around 2780 BC and medical textbooks in 1557 BC. Greek civilization did not exist during those dates. Greece emerged in human history around 800 BC. Most of the early Greeks scholars and philosophers were educated in Egypt.

African American students were not completing degree programs at Sinclair due in part to the lies in the textbooks and courses. Mwawaza Sanyika, a student in my African American Psychology class, organized BOTIN to train peers in rites of passage. The program was modeled after Simba Na Malaika Wachanga (SNMW) founded during the Black Power era. The organization promoted programs in Detroit, Chicago, St. Louis, and with Mwawaza's leadership, Dayton. He asked me to become a Rafiki (friend) of SNMW.

"What does a Rafiki do in this organization?"

"Rafiki attends SNMW conventions and supports the work and mission of the organization." He also suggested that I consider training to become a Simba.

I expressed my interest, and in a year, the student, Mwawaza, became my teacher.

In 1993, we created the Dayton Rites of Passage Program and trained youth in West Dayton and Middletown, Ohio. We presented our training methods and program at the National Black Studies Association in Atlanta and conducted workshops for social workers of medically fragile foster care children.

We trained youth in the Ujima Network of West Dayton. We met with twelve to fifteen youths, male and female, ages ten to fifteen. We introduced them to the customs and technology of SNMW. Some of the customs introduced were greeting each other, standing with shoulders erect, and tabura (African discipline). In this program, youth learned how to apply the seven principles of Kwanzaa in role plays and visual art activities. They learned what it was to become an adult, leadership skills, and basic Swahili phrases. My sons, Emman and Dakona, also trained in SNMW.

We received funding from Good Samaritan Hospital and created the Dayton Mentorship Program in 1998. This program focused on violence prevention. More than fifty youths were trained with the SNMW rites of passage and technology. The program created youth leaders, who assisted with the training and recruitment. We moved to three locations within West Dayton to improve program recruitment and retention. We used digital cameras and computers to make films and videos as alternatives to violent images shown on the news, TV, and films. Youth created songs, games, and videos to promote good behaviors. Youth leaders received stipends to reinforce their commitment in the program. Youth from different neighborhoods built relationships and friendships.

In 2000, Douglas Edwards of SNMW, a teacher in the Atlanta Public Schools system, created Alliance of Black Leadership and Education (ABLE) Youth Leadership Institute. He created a curriculum to overcome the resistance public schools had toward our Pan-African rites of passage curricula. I explained the curriculum to the principal of Colonial White High School, Mr. Griffin, and got his support to launch ABLE.

Fifteen male juniors and seniors were recruited to inaugurate the program. These young men were introduced to core characteristics of leadership, lessons of humbleness, mastering of emotions, acquiring knowledge, and African discipline (tabura).

At the first meeting, I asked, "Who are you? Why are you here? What did you bring?"

Most of them were unclear about their identity, purpose, and hidden talents. This ABLE group hosted a Black History Month program and a Pre-Kwanzaa celebration in December.

I introduced ABLE to students at Sinclair. We trained about ten students in ABLE's curriculum of leadership development and cultural knowledge. We started a mentoring program at Arlington Courts, a notorious public-housing project, after four African American youths were killed in a weekend. One of those murdered was a female who lived in the community. We visited her mother, offered our sympathy, and asked her permission to hold a prayer vigil for her daughter. At the vigil, we committed to begin a violence prevention program at Arlington Courts.

ABLE initiated and ran a violence prevention program for about eighteen months. More than twenty-five youths, from eight to fifteen, were mentored, encouraged, and taken on field trips to experience life beyond the 'hood. ABLE originated the Dayton Youth Violence Prevention Task Force, which involved City Commissioner Dean Lovelace, the police chief, a juvenile judge, and a clergyman. Youth were trained to model prosocial behaviors and provide Pan-African leadership for their peers. We organized vigils for the victims of Black-on-Black violence and created programs in the neighborhoods where these acts of violence occurred.

For two years, the task force met monthly at Dayton City Hall discussing ways to combine our individual programs to better address youth violence. I proposed a downtown office to serve as headquarters for youth leaders to implement violence prevention activities. Since the city was unwilling to fund the project and we had no source of funding, the task force disbanded.

ABLE trained leaders of Sinclair's African American Culture Club. Many of these youth leaders created careers using the ABLE training as a foundation. The following list notes some ABLE leaders and their accomplishments:

- Toccara Jones developed a career as an international model and reality show star.
- Lamarr Lewis is a therapist, certified mental health counselor, and entrepreneur.
- Bakari Lumumba completed his masters in African American Studies at Ohio University and began his doctorate at The Ohio State University.
- Shaquanna Metcalf created a career in community service and public relations.
- Stephanie Motley is an occupational therapist assistant who works with elders in nursing homes.
- Candace Reed launched an event planning business.
- Chad Sloss is a college instructor working on his doctorate in sociology at the University of Cincinnati.
- Emman Twe created Digital Good Times, a technology and music company.

I met an ABLE leader who had been in and out of homeless shelters. He said that he kept up with other ABLE leaders on Facebook and was trying to get back in college. Despite these challenges, I observed his ongoing recovery and demonstration that ABLE affected his life.

Boikai S. Twe

Chapter 15

Black Lives Matter

"I shot the sheriff...in self-defense."
— Bob Marley

On August 5, 2014, John Crawford III was shot and killed by police officers. He walked through Walmart in Beavercreek, a suburb of Dayton. He spoke on his phone while holding a BB gun he picked up from the store shelf.

Amaha Sellassie had just completed African American Studies with me and was moved by the murder. He and the Ohio Students Association organized to seek justice for John Crawford using the Black Lives Matter Network.

The first John Crawford March for Justice started at the Beavercreek Walmart. The Dayton Africana Elders Council was asked to participate. Jessie Gooden, a veteran leader of the Civil Rights Movement, Nzipo Glenn, an exiled representative of the Pan-African Congress of Azina, South Africa, and I shared our experiences in the struggle for justice.

The youth leaders asked, "How long should we wage this struggle for justice?" "How should we interact with the news media?" "How should we prepare for this long walk to justice?"

I shared my experience as the organizer of the Dayton Youth Violence Prevention Task Force. I offered leadership training and an understanding of the steps to power.

The Grand Jury of Greene County failed to indict the police who murdered John Crawford III, which happened about four days before the murder of Michael Brown in Ferguson, Missouri.

The Ferguson Uprising led to widespread rioting, police violence, looting, gunfire, and propelled the Black Lives Matter (BLM) Network into the international spotlight. Three hundred twenty-one people were arrested during the unrest. Mama Nzipo Glenn and I went to Ferguson to stand with protesters in front of the police station. Warned that the police could arrest us for protesting in front of their headquarters, we stood our ground. An around-the-clock protest for justice for Michael Brown continued for almost two months.

A second March for Justice for John Crawford was held at the Beavercreek Walmart to advocate for police reform. At the beginning of the march, I poured libation for Black lives lost to police and community violence. I asked the marchers to remember the Black lives lost in the Transatlantic Slave Trade, American enslavement, Civil Rights and Black Power struggles, and those murdered in our neighborhoods. I reminded them that the "hotter the battle, the sweeter the victory." I asked them to face the reality that we are at war for truth and justice. We cannot run away from emancipating ourselves from mental slavery and systematic racism.

Amaha Sellassie became a leader of the movement for justice for John Crawford in Ohio, a community organizer in West Dayton, and an assistant professor of sociology at Sinclair. The struggle for justice and freedom from White supremacy since these events led to more weeping, wailing, and looting. I cautioned Amaha against being fooled by his peers to put his life and career on the line by becoming the spokesperson for the movement. I encouraged him to adopt the leadership style of Harriet Tubman and Ella Jo Baker, whose focus was on emancipating Africans versus fighting racism. He went on to head the completion of Gem City Market, built to remedy the food desert in West Dayton.

The BLM movement began in 2013 after George Zimmerman was acquitted for the shooting death of Trayvon Martin. Following the deaths of Michael Brown and Eric Garner in New York City, BLM's street protests garnered international exposure. Three African American women—Alicia Garza, Patrisse Cullors, and Opal Tometi—originated the movement, which became more prominent after the murder of George Floyd on Africa Day, May 25, 2020. As captured on a cellphone camera, a White Minneapolis, Minnesota police officer, Derek Chauvin, knelt on Floyd's neck for almost nine minutes.

African emancipation from systematic racism is a global movement due to the ongoing murders of Black people by police and vigilantes. However, Black-on-Black murders and crimes against Black women have not received the same attention. Black Studies courses have been the only spaces where this issue has been studied. We must defend ourselves against miseducation (internal racism) to avoid self-destruction, colorism, and patriarchy. Discipline and self-control are essential for our destiny.

The miseducation of Africans by systematic racism has led to global trauma and violence. High levels of Black-on-Black violence and patriarchy exist in South Africa, Brazil, the U.S.A, and the U.K, alongside systematic racism. When Blacks are pushed into the abyss of poverty and miseducation, the reaction is often self-destruction and suicide. About 800,000 Africans were murdered by other

Africans as internalized racism permeated the Rwanda genocide of 1994. Internalized violence and miseducation resulted in the deaths of more than 250,000 Liberians in that country's civil war.

The Haitian Revolution was a successful confrontation with African enslavement and White domination. It began in 1791 and ended in 1804 when Haiti became a sovereign state. This confrontation of White terror created fear and retaliation from France, Britain, and the U.S. This revolution demonstrated to Africans and the world that enslaved people could free themselves by force. The story of African emancipation was also reinforced during the American Civil War when almost 200,000 Africans fought with the Union Army and Navy to defeat the Confederate State of America.

Africans' determination to be sovereign people was seen in the First Italo-Ethiopian War from 1895 to 1896. At the Battle of Adowa, Ethiopian forces defeated the Italian invading forces. This demonstrated to Europeans that Africans were willing and able to fight for freedom. Ethiopia became a Pan-African symbol of the struggle to maintain our freedom and human dignity. The first Pan-African Conference was held in 1900 with representatives from Ethiopia and Liberia, the two remaining sovereign states after the European scramble for Africa.

Fights against White terror and colonization occurred in the 1950s and 1960s when the American Civil Rights and African Liberation Movements emerged. These movements reduced the "legal" murders and massacres of Black lives across the globe through national laws and human rights agreements at the United Nations. The equality of Black lives was projected in the Black Arts and Black Power Movements of the 1960s. The struggle for human rights and against White-male domination demonstrated our value for sovereignty and human dignity.

For our lives to truly matter, we must have faith in our parents, teachers, leaders, culture, and righteousness and victory of our struggle.

Boikai S. Twe

Chapter 16

Economic Community of West Africa and African Union

"If you like yourself, people will like you."
— Ewe proverb

June 2017, the Heads of State of the Economic Community of West Africa (ECOWAS) met in Monrovia, Liberia for the first time in three decades. This meeting occurred in the final year of Ellen Johnson-Sirleaf's reign as President of Liberia and Chairperson of ECOWAS. This meeting was to further the ECOWAS agenda for economic integration, peace and stability, democratic governance, and implementing common currency in West Africa. The Israeli Prime Minister, Benjamin Netanyahu, and King Hussein of Morocco asked to attend. Israel was interested in strengthening relations with West Africa and Morocco requested to join ECOWAS, indicators of the organization's success in leading the African Union toward regional integration and economic unification.

An achievement of President William R. Tolbert of Liberia was his central role in the establishment of ECOWAS in the 1970s. President Sirleaf's chairpersonship demonstrated the drive toward gender equality, credible elections, and improved relationship with industrialized nations.

Improvement in West African leadership was what I called for in *Which Way Liberia: The Gun or the Book?* I published this booklet in 2005 stating that West African leaders "should not be 'gravy seekers, self-colonizers or lone rangers' who are out to gain recognition and steal as much as they can. They should demonstrate commitment to ECOWAS and Pan-Africanism."

Some leaders of ECOWAS moved away from selfishness and greed unlike former leaders including Charles Taylor of Liberia, Gnassingbe Eyadema of Togo, and Yahya Jammeh of the Gambia. However, ECOWAS is still faced with Boko Haram in Nigeria and Cameroon, post-traumatic disorder of civil wars in Liberia, Sierra Leone, Ivory Coast, and Guinea, and widespread governance corruption. I wrote that the self-destruction in West Africa was the result of its leaders "conspiring with others to worship money, status, violence, and Christian and Muslim values while destroying African spiritual, cultural, and natural resources and traditions." Leaders of ECOWAS must not glorify the region's colonial history and economic dependency, and instead strive for regional integration and economic self-determination and cooperation.

A common West African passport and free movement in the region are applauded; however, more needs to be done to improve regional integration, rural development, and reduction in corruption. The increasing urbanization of West Africans contributes to poverty, diseases, and the loss of community. Living in urban neighborhoods as renters or squatters is not the same as living in village communities on communal land. Youth are increasingly alienated from communities stirring a need for cultural education in these urban centers. The need to focus on the development of people, especially women and children in urban and rural areas of West Africa, is prevalent.

A strong African cultural identity should be promoted in homes, schools, and places of worship to counteract the destruction of our cultural unity by Christian and Muslim fundamentalism. African cultural identity can be described by five traits:

1. Divinity: the interrelationship between each person and the divine force (God) in the universe.
2. Teachability: the capacity to know, understanding, and sharing knowledge and wisdom.
3. Perfectibility: the transformative process of the human spirit that is in a perpetual state of improvement.
4. Free Will: the capacity to make conscious, deliberate choices to respond to one's reality.
5. Moral and social responsibility: a mandate to create moral and ethical relations with others without sacrificing national security.

West Africans need to cultivate a common heritage and humanity that will defend us against terrorists, thieves and liars who claim to be friends and saviors.

President William V.S. Tubman of Liberia played a key role in establishing the Organization of African Unity (OAU) in 1963 on May 25 (Africa Day). Thirty-two African states committed to strive for unity and liberation from colonialism. Tubman headed the Monrovia Group with twenty-two states that wanted a slow move to unity. Nkrumah headed the Casablanca Group with seven states that wanted a quick move to the United States of Africa.

With backing from the US, the Monrovia Group won, and Africa lost the opportunity for a swift transition to African Union.

I witnessed these meetings of African heads of state in Monrovia. We were released early from school to greet these dignitaries. We stood on the sidewalk chanting "Akwaaba Kwame Nkrumah!" which translates to Welcome, Kwame Nkrumah. Teachers taught on the meetings and agreements to establish the OAU. Hosted by Emperor Haile Selassie I, the first summit was held in Addis Ababa, Ethiopia. The vision of Pan-Africanism that brought this historic event into reality was created in Liberia and the African diaspora by scholars like Edward W. Blyden, Alexander Crummell, Martin Delany, and W.E.B Du Bois.

In 1920, Marcus Garvey created Pan-African projects within the Universal Negro Improvement Association (UNIA). He established the Black Star Line shipping company in New York to promote trade and repatriation of Africans back to Africa. He planned to create African American resettlements in Liberia, Ethiopia, and the Congo. He advocated for a centralized government for Africa and its people in the diaspora. These projects inspired young leaders like Kwame Nkrumah, Nnamdi Azikiwe, and Jomo Kenyatta to return to Africa to fight for liberation from European colonialism and promote an African union.

In October 1963, Emperor Haile Selassie I spoke to the United Nation General Assembly recounting Ethiopia's experience of racism with the League of Nations. He said:

> "Last May, in Addis Ababa, I convened a meeting of Heads of African States and Governments. In three days, the thirty-two nations represented at that conference

demonstrated to the world that when the will and the determination exist, nations and peoples of diverse backgrounds can and will work together. In unity, to the achievement of common goals and the assurance of equality and brotherhood which we desire. On the question of racial discrimination, the Addis Ababa Conference taught, to those who will learn this further lesson:

- That until the philosophy which holds one race superior and another inferior is finally and permanently discredited and abandoned;
- That until there are no longer first-class and second-class citizens of any nation;
- That until the color of a man's skin is of no more significance than the color of his eyes;
- That until the basic human rights are equally guaranteed to all without regard to race;
- That until that day, the dream of lasting peace and world citizenship and the rule of international morality will remain but a fleeting illusion, to be pursued but never attained;
- And until the ignoble and unhappy regimes that hold our brothers in Angola, in Mozambique and in South Africa in subhuman bondage have been toppled and destroyed;
- Until bigotry and prejudice and malicious and inhuman self-interest have been replaced by understanding and tolerance

and good-will;
- Until Africans stand and speak as free beings, equal in the eyes of all men, as they are in the eyes of Heaven;
- Until that day, the African continent will not know peace. We Africans will fight, if necessary, and we know that we shall win, as we are confident in the victory of good over evil."[28]

This speech inspired Bob Marley's hit 1977 song *War*.

In 2002, the Organization of African Unity became the African Union (AU) in Durban, South Africa. AU is headquartered in Addis Ababa. It consists of fifty-five African states organized into six regional communities like ECOWAS. The sixth region of Africa is the diaspora. It adopted a flag with a green sun setting on a green field. Golden stars, one for each represented state, surround the sun. It created a Pan-African Parliament. In 2013, it adopted a fifty-year plan—Agenda 2063—to mark its half-century of existence. This agenda has seven aspirations:

1. A prosperous Africa based on inclusive growth and sustainable development
2. An integrated continent, politically united, based on Pan-Africanism and the vision of Africa's Renaissance
3. An Africa of good governance, democracy, respect for human rights, justice, and the rule of law

---

[28] "Read Emperor Haile Selassie's Iconic 1963 Speech that Inspired Bob Marley's Hit Song 'War'." *Face2Face Africa,* 21 May 2018, https://face2face.com/article/read-emperor-haile-selassies-iconic-1963-speech-that-inspired-bob-marleys-hit-song-war.

4. A peaceful and secure Africa
5. An Africa with a strong cultural identity, common heritage, values, and ethics
6. An Africa whose development is people driven, especially women, youth, and children
7. An Africa as a strong, united, and influential global player and partner

Being part of the diaspora, the Rastafari community is committed to Pan-Africanism and African spirituality. We embraced Emperor Haile Selassie I as the king of kings, lord of lords, and conquering lion of Judah. We see the African Union as a symbolic and concrete structure of African aspirations and legacy. The African Union is our creation and salvation. It must be reformed to provide greater freedom and security to Africans. African psychology can contribute to this reform and the liberation of the African mind, character, and the illumination of the African spirit according to the mission statement of The Association of Black Psychologists.[29]

---

[29] Rowe, Taasogle Daryl. "Psychology International Newsletter". Mar. 2015.

Chapter 17

Building for Eternity

"Living is worthless for one without a home."
—Ethiopian proverb

In 2006, my brother, Alex, retired as an architect employed by the City of New York. He returned to Monrovia to create Kiara Development Corporation (KDC), a firm created to design and rebuild Liberia. My brothers, Francis, Charles, and I invested more than $20,000 in this venture.

Alex's experience did not prepare him for the construction industry in Liberia. His first year in business left him in debt and without a prospect of maintaining the firm.

As chairperson of the board of directors, I said, "Why do we have thirty employees on payroll? Most of them are doing nothing but collecting a paycheck."

Alex said, "It is hard to find and keep good tradesmen. I want the capacity to complete a variety of projects."

One of his biggest mistakes was hiring too many full-time employees which bloated expenses when we had few ongoing construction projects.

"Consider reducing your workforce. Since you haven't had many jobs, the payroll deficit is only growing. We cannot keep operating in the hole with employees or suppliers. We need to reduce expenses and find ways to increase KDC's income."

He subcontracted parts of existing projects to reduce expenses.

KDC faced competition from Lebanese contractors who dominated the Liberian construction industry. They supplied building materials and contractors. Through their ability to pay huge bribes, acquire capital, and loans, they controlled the industry. This monopoly of power and resources had a negative effect on Liberia's economy and future.

In Africa's construction history, architects, builders, and tradespeople were also the priests and custodians of the projects they built. The Chinese recently entered the Liberian construction industry to create Chinese architecture. A building reflects the creativity and spirit of the builders. It is often invested with cultural memories and spiritual significance.

KDC completed more than forty projects and strives to provide dividends to its investors. A recently completed project was the design and construction of the African Methodist Episcopal University Graduate School in Monrovia. This project took two years to complete. The quality of the firm's work has been the primary marketing tool. Striving for excellence to build for eternity, self-determination, and employing local tradespeople have provided solid footings for this venture.

The psychology of construction is vital to the expansion of African psychology. Creating superstructures to provide homes for our ideas, memories, and families or spaces to conduct business and worship is essential for competence and security. My contribution to the reconstruction of Brewerville is building a KDC-designed home on a lot my mother gave me.

The lot had some environmental challenges because it's one of the major drains for excess water. I had to find a way to redirect the storm water that floods the property during the rainy season. KDC designed and built a drainage system that reduced the flow of water on the property and elevated the foundation. Redesigning projects to accommodate the environment has been an ongoing cause for costs overrun.

Building for eternity involves adjusting to changing circumstances without losing integrity and function. A construction must be anchored on secure footings much like African psychology provides footings for life and development. Otherwise, we are anchored in other people's constructions and realities.

Adjustments were made on two other projects I worked with others to construct. The first one was the Harambee Coffee Roasters Cooperative. Large numbers of refugees from Rwanda and South Sudan resettled in Dayton. This migration motivated the city to create a Welcome Dayton Initiative to assist with resettlement and integration. Members of the African community decided to create a coffee-roasters cooperative to support economic integration for the new immigrants.

The American Friends Service Committee of Dayton contributed a business plan to purchase a roaster and open a coffee shop where fair trade African coffee would be roasted and sold.

"Dr. Twe, will you be our interim president of the board of directors?"

I hesitated to respond. I was not a coffee drinker and knew little about the industry. "Yes, I will head the project until I retire and return to Monrovia." I committed to learn about the coffee industry.

The project was revised when we could not raise $200,000 to launch the business. A few committed African immigrants with skills in not-for-profit organizations helped us create a strategic plan to sell fair trade Ethiopian coffee in 2016.

We sought to maintain the footings (goals) of this social enterprise. As president of the board of directors, I led an adjustment to maintain our values for fair trade, self-determination, and community. For two years, we sold one-pound bags of Ethiopian coffee at community events. Consumers loved our product, but we lacked the capacity to hire employees, which is essential to building for eternity.

The second project that needed adjustments was the creation of the Dayton Africana Elders Council. The concept of the council came from Marlon Shackelford and students who had taken Africana Studies with me. They worked with the Dayton African American Cultural Festival which established an African Village. They wanted the African Village to play a greater role in the festival and the community.

In 2013, Marlon Shackelford and Amaha Sellassie, my former student and Rasta brother, approached me about creating an elders council.

I said, "How will elders be recruited to form this council?"

"We already contacted some outstanding elders in the community. Can you draft the mission statement and create a structure for the council?"

I worked with Pastor Robert Jones to draft a mission statement. Once approved by the organizing committee, we created a process and program to induct members into the council.

The varying professional backgrounds and perspectives

of the recruited elders presented challenges and opportunities to create a superstructure. The original fifteen members of the council included a physician, a judge, two pastors, a retired law professor, a visual artist/educator, a college professor, president of the Dayton Branch of the Association for the Study of African American Life and History (ASALH), a retired civil rights leader, a former Pan-African Congress representative and the historian of Dayton's African American community. We agreed to use the Nguzo Saba (Seven Principles) of Kwanzaa to provide the foundation for this superstructure. We agreed that the council should have a balance of male and female members.

We created an age-grade African Village substructure:

- Elders Council for senior grade members over 60 years old
- Nation Builders for members 40-59 years old
- Warriors, 20-39 years old, were expected to organize and socialize the adolescents in the village.

The Dayton Africana Elders Council organized in an organic way to prepare next generations.

As a co-facilitator, I was often asked, "What is the structure and constitution of the council?"

"The council operates on consensus and uses the Nguzo Saba to guide its mission and goals. It evolves to better address the needs of our senior members, adults, and youth who are socialized to replace us."

Building for eternity involves collective work and a diversity of tradespeople. Moreover, it requires the construction to be a good fit to stand the test of time. African constructions are some of the oldest superstructures on the face of the earth. They were built with local materials and skills to be environmentally and spiritually relevant.

African psychology is deconstructing, reconstructing, and constructing ideas, memories and practices that will maintain African self-consciousness and self-extension. The price and commitment of construction are high if we seek to build for eternity.

Chapter 18

Vulnerable and Empowered

"The one who itches is the one who scratches."
—Tanzanian proverb

Estimating the vulnerability of Africans is difficult. However, African psychology teaches that a way to measure the success of a society is how it cares for the most vulnerable. Many are susceptible to poverty, civil crisis, human trafficking, unemployment, and poor education. Vulnerability is evidenced in the millions of Africans in refugee camps and those risking their lives to cross the Mediterranean Sea. From 2014-2020, thousands died trying to migrate to Europe.[30] Civil crisis and terrorism in Nigeria, Libya, Somalia, Central African Republic, South Sudan, and the Democratic Republic of the Congo increased vulnerability.

African refugees and displaced people are vulnerable to mental and physical abuses, and disconnection from family. They lack the means to control their movements and living spaces. In 2017, African migrants to Libya were sold as slaves by warring militias.[31] Combined with external influences from Euro-American and Arab lies, the state of

---

[30] International Organization for Migration, https://missingmigrants.iom.int.
[31] Youssef, Nour. "Sale of Migrants as Slaves in Libya Causes Outrage in Africa and Paris." *The New York Times*, 19 Nov. 2017.

insecurity and inferiority can seem insurmountable.

European and American media highlight the tragedies of Africa, but seldom mention their roles in creating them. They do not explain how enslavement and exploitation formed their wealth and power. They do not explain how African states were destabilized and why leaders like Patrice Lumumba, Kwame Nkrumah, Thomas Sankara, and Muammar Al Gaddafi were ousted. The propaganda of media, missionaries, and education makes us vulnerable to lies and deception.

In Monrovia, this social crisis can be seen with the zogo children. These homeless youth try to survive in the forest, cemeteries, and on the streets. Some make a living as motorbike drivers, others as petty criminals and beggars. Many cope with mental disorders triggered by war trauma with drugs. Desperation is prevalent.

They rob the dead in cemeteries and the living at markets. Tiles on the graves of my stepfather and brother were sold as scrap. The zogo boys in central Monrovia target foreigners or Liberians just returning from the United States. Their strategy is to harass you for money until you concede.

"Daddy, your son hungry."

If you do not respond with money, they follow you to plead their case.

"Daddy, your children hungry and want small thing to eat."

To get rid of them, you have to give them Liberian dollars or become aggressive. The zogo children reflect the social vulnerability of the Liberian population after civil war and twelve years of President Ellen Johnson Sirleaf's rule. I have nephews who are zogos.

I experienced vulnerability on July 13, 2017. I had enjoyed dinner at a neighborhood restaurant near St. Paul

Bridge. A petty criminal on a motorbike rode by, snatched my wallet from my shirt pocket and disappeared into the darkness. Not only did he get all the money I had for a trip to Accra, Ghana, he had my credit cards and green card.

I reported the robbery to the police.

The officer said, "We do not have a police car to pursue criminals or a computer to write the report. If you give me a few dollars I can have a report for you tomorrow."

Without a completed report, I left frustrated and disappointed in the civil servant.

The next day, I borrowed $20 from a friend. I repeated the process of sitting and waiting to get the report written and sent to the Liberian National Police Central Office. Robbed twice in less than twenty-four hours.

Without access to money and my green card, I could not reenter the U.S. I sought to secure travel documents from the U.S. Consulate in Monrovia but was informed that I had to wait more than four weeks to meet anyone who could assist me. Vulnerability and helplessness contributed to depression and high levels of stress. The experience helped me realize how challenging it is to deal with a loss of resources and control.

My mother was ninety-one-years old and no longer able to care for herself. Her inability to get out of bed and move around her house brought on isolation and depression.

One sunny day, I asked, "Do you want to go to the beach?"

"Yes."

Alex, Emman, and I took her to the beach. She beamed with joy to be out of confinement. We drove to the beach and placed her in her wheelchair. With cooling beverages and an oversized umbrella, Emman recorded an interview with her. We enjoyed the breeze from the Atlantic Ocean; however, her freedom was short-lived.

I realized that restrictions of poverty and weak social organizations can lead to stress and mental disorders. The zogo children represent people who are vulnerable because we accepted lies that we are incompetent and cannot take care of ourselves.

African leaders and professionals have to do a better job of defying the lies that we need Euro-American and Asian cultures to save us from incompetence. Africans need social services and empowerment to offset the recklessness and frustration created by vulnerability.

Social workers need to empower these groups by organizing intergenerational interactions and improving their social skills. We should seek ways to engage zogo boys and girls in decision-making and policies affecting them. They need to better organize and get the recognition they deserve as voters who helped get President George Weah elected in Liberia. The president grew up in Clara Town, a shantytown of Monrovia. His rise to the presidency inspired slum dwellers and vulnerable youth to identify with his story. We need interactions and lessons from Pan-African professionals and elders. We can save ourselves if we emancipate from inferiority and incompetence.

The lack of organization, commitment, and competence contributes to the vulnerability. It took seven days to get the police report. Each day I went to the sub-station to push and pay the Liberian National Police Central Office to give me temporary approval to travel, I had to document the robbery with a report.

Because I had no faith in the police, I traveled to criminal hangouts and motorbike stations offering a reward for the return of my stolen documents. African institutions must be better organized and competent to meet the needs of citizens.

A visible sign of women emancipation and competence in Monrovia was the work of Mary Broh, former interim mayor. She demonstrated her competence and emancipation from the lies of inferiority in every position she served. The first Saturday of each month was dedicated to community cleanup and named Mary Broh Day in her honor.

She set high standards for the community-delivered services that influenced Monrovia and the nation. President Ellen Johnson-Sirleaf often dispatched her to troubleshoot and reorganize government agencies and services. She was a solid leader in the midst of incompetence and disorganization. Unable to accept corruption, she confronted it and was resigned to a new position. Her absence was felt when garbage accumulated on the streets of Monrovia for more than two months.

Moving from vulnerability to empowerment is a lesson taught by several African leaders. Emperor Haile Selassie I regained Ethiopia's sovereignty after the Italian invasion and destruction of the country from 1936 to 1941. He used Ethiopia's cultural history and diplomatic relationships to press for Africa's independence and unification. African youth and elders have been empowered by Selassie's work to make Addis Ababa the headquarters of the African Union and to see God as Black acting on behalf of oppressed people.

After serving twenty-five years in prison, President Nelson Mandela became the first democratically elected president of South Africa in 1994. He emancipated himself and empowered the world to focus on inclusion and African self-rule.

President Ellen Johnson-Sirleaf came from political exile

and defeat during the 1990s to become Africa's first democratically elected female Head of State in 2005. She empowered the women of Liberia, Africa, and the world to see themselves as capable and determined as men.

President George Weah was born in Monrovia. He grew up in Clara Town where he played football, American soccer. He did not complete high school until later in his adult life. He became Africa's top football player and the 1995 World Player of the Year. In 2005, he ran for president and lost to Ellen Johnson-Sirleaf. In 2014, he was elected to the Senate of Liberia. Three years later, he was elected as the 25th president of Liberia and has served since 2018. His rags-to-riches story inspires vulnerable Liberians and Africans to dream of personal empowerment and wealth.

Chapter 19

Making Music

"In an abundance of water, the fool is thirsty."
—Ethiopian proverb

My first memory of making music was when my first brother, Alex, was born. At four-years old, I banged on the bottom of a zinc tub. My grandmother scolded me for making "noise." It may have been my way of celebrating his arrival. My second memory of music was a rites of initiation. Young girls sang as adult women played the sasaa. Also called shekere, this West African percussion instrument is a dried gourd with a netted covering of woven beads or cowries. These early memories continue to shape feelings about music.

African music is unique. Its repeated patterns establish beats and changes to demonstrate freedom and creativity. It has a conversational quality where different instruments and voices engage in lively exchanges. This call-and-response pattern is seen in singing, drumming, and dancing in today's musical culture. The participation brings people together who may have no other way to communicate.

African popular music is a blend of African, European, African American, and Middle Eastern music. In the West, this blend of the music is called world music because it is the musical vocabulary and memory of the modern world.

Without it, we may not be able to survive and flourish in the "concrete jungle." African music is the driving force for freedom and justice in the world.

My early experience did not give me any confidence that I could make music until I was in high school. I tried out—and was selected—for the school choir. Since I considered myself a scholar and not a singer, I was surprised I was chosen. The choir director asked me to sing solos during rehearsals and concerts.

Classmates, Louis McClain and Sarr McClain, said to me, "Let's create a singing group that can compete with other groups on campus."

We agreed to call the group "Lovin' Breeds." We rehearsed in the dorm room and performed at campus talent shows. We experienced the joy and discipline of performing music.

I also tried out for the cultural dance troupe on campus. This troupe was an attempt by the Ministry of Cultural Affairs to introduce Liberian traditional music and dance to campus life. I did not do well in these rehearsals, so I focused on the school choir and singing group. We created matching outfits and sang popular songs. Our performances at talent shows gave us a reputation as singers on and off campus. After graduation, I was asked to join a dance band in Monrovia. I did not have the interest or musical skills needed, so I declined.

Professional musicians play a crucial role in African societies. During major milestones, musicians played the role of griots in the transmission of knowledge and memories. Musicians perform lullabies, game songs, initiation rites, weddings, funerals, and ceremonies for ancestors. Some musicians have the reputation of being lazy, demanding, and irresponsible.

Grona Boy Go Zion

A musician who had a profound effect on me was Fela Anikulapo-Kuti. His style of music, Afrobeat, was influenced by African American jazz and the Black Power Movement. His song, "Black Man's Cry", was released in 1971, the year I graduated from high school.

Another music maker who grabbed my attention was Manu Dibango and his song "Soul Makossa". This blend of music was funky, timeless, and could be heard in most Black nightclubs and on Black radio. I felt like Africa was with me in America.

Bob Marley and the Wailers was another musical group who penetrated my mind and liberated my spirit. In 1974, I heard the first Bob Marley song, "I Shot the Sheriff", a hit covered by Eric Clapton. This song reminded me of my grona-boy days on the streets of Monrovia. *Catch a Fire*, their first album, contained hits like "Concrete Jungle", "Stir It Up", "No More Trouble", and "Slave Driver". Their 1978 *Exodus Tour* was one of the most memorable concerts I ever experienced. The audience stood the entire performance.

The music of Bob Marley and the Wailers became a cornerstone of 21st-century music. His songs have been covered by countless singers and quoted by many hip-hop performers, including my sons, Emman (Small Eyez) and Dakona (Awful Truth). In the 2014 *Rolling Stone Special Edition: Bob Marley, His 50 Greatest Songs*, Will Hermes wrote,

> "His artistic fearlessness and social commitment remain an inspiration to activists, musical and otherwise. His songs of freedom have become universal hymns."

The songs of Bob Marley and the Wailers brought me into the spiritual community of Rastafari.

My next encounter with music-making occurred in 1978

when I met Antonio "LA" Reid. We collected scrap paper and busted bales of paper bags as employees of Duro Paper Bag Factory. When we discovered that we lived in the Faye Public Housing Project in Cincinnati, Ohio, we decided to ride to work together.

In route to work one day, we listened to WEBN, a Cincinnati radio station. The station supported local bands by airing original compilations.

LA said, "That's our song playing." LA was the drummer and leader of a local band, Essence. Their first song to make the airwaves, "Wake Up", filled the car. He became a great music maker and producer with his partner, Babyface.

When "gangsta rap" took over urban music culture, we discussed its influence on Black culture.

I said, "Don't follow this trend. This is bad for our culture."

"This music is selling."

"You can make big money selling positive songs of Black culture." I gave him some of my writings and other literature of Black culture. He discovered and produced some of the greatest acts in pop music history including Toni Braxton, Kanye West, Rihanna, TLC, Outkast, Goodie Mob, Mariah Carey, Pink, Justin Bieber, and Usher.

In his 2016 autobiography, *Sing to Me*, he stated that I introduced him to Bob Marley and books that transformed his thinking about himself and his music. In this book he wrote,

> "I'd always felt guilty that I didn't have a formal education, so I devoured the books Winston gave me. I loved listening to him speak in his velvet tones and elegant language.

> With his help, I started to see, for the first time, that I was smart."

He celebrated his fiftieth birthday in New York. The party was emceed by Jay-Z and attended by Oprah, Beyoncé, and Rihanna.

He said to me, "You've been a guru to me since we met in Cincinnati."

I was surprised that he saw our relationship in this manner.

In 1983, I was a DJ in Cincinnati bars to spread the message of reggae. Yahmin Tafari and I promoted reggae across the city. Cincinnati attracted some of the best international reggae acts. I saw Peter Tosh, Big Youth, Steel Pulse, I-Threes, and the Wailers at Bogart's, which is still a venue for reggae acts.

My younger brother, Albert Dehconte Nyepan Gibson, was another music maker influenced by my musical interest. Dehconte was the only trained musician in our family. He earned his undergraduate degree at Southern University School of Music and Fine Arts. He was a performing artist who sang and played several instruments. He completed three albums of world music: *Liberian Libation*, *Do You Feel Me?*, and *Organic Afro Soul*. The latter album was dedicated to me as his guru. We had lengthy discussions about the music business and trends. His travels to Puerto Rico and Brazil influenced his music-making and spirituality. He died unexpectedly on July 2, 2016.

My sons, Emman, Dakona and Armah (Thomas Massaquoi) sought careers in the music industry, due in part to their Uncle Dehconte and my relationship with LA Reid. They are more musically talented than I, as they create music that reflects social consciousness and commitment. Their projects have influenced family, friends, and communities across the globe.

In recent years, I have played the shekere at cultural events. Initially, I was reluctant to play this instrument because it is primarily played by women in Liberia. I overcame my reluctance and joined African community drummers to play at cultural celebrations like Kwanzaa.

At my Aunt Lenora Zena Holcombe's home going service, I played the shekere and read a poem she gave me sixteen years prior. In tribute to my ancestors and her work, she trained young girls at the Liberian National Cultural Center — I offered the musical libation. Music is a medium of healing, celebration, liberation, and gaining access to higher power and collective memories.

Chapter 20

Libation to Ancestors

"Do not count on the protection of other people's ancestor spirits."
— African proverb

Pouring libation is an African ritual used as a sacred offering to honor and remember ancestors. The ritual was written about and performed by ancient Africans in Egypt. It takes many forms, but the most popular is the pouring of water or liquid on the ground. Among many ethnic groups of Africa, water is a sacred symbol of ancestors and God. One can observe libations and prayers along the rivers and beaches of Africa.

At the annual convention for the Association of Black Psychologists, I participated in this ritual to honor the ancestors of the association. No other professional conference or gathering that I attended used this ritual. The demonstration shows that African psychologists deem this ritual essential to well-being and righteous living. I observed and participated in this ritual in Liberia and began performing libation in 1990 when I first celebrated Kwanzaa.

Kwanzaa is the African American holiday which celebrates family, culture, and community. Libation is rooted in our concern with eloquence, unity, and stability. When confronted with problems or tasks, we use libation to ask our ancestors for a solution or redress. When we experience peace, success, or prosperity, we express gratitude to our ancestors with libation. Libation can be used to ask for more goodness, abundant food, solidarity, and security. As an elder, I have been asked to pour libation at family meetings, community events, and funerals.

Libation is a reminder that life has a divine higher order. In ancient Egypt, this higher order was a combination of justice and truth, called Ma'at. The path to eternal life was morality. Libation performed by elders or priests was invented to assist the dead to attain eternity. Only through moral living of justice and truth can one attain divinity. During this ritual, the community is reminded of the moral deeds of the ancestors to provide models for others to follow. To acknowledge these deeds, the elder or priest uses the power and beauty of words to remind living relatives of their kinship with Ma'at (Truth and Justice), a way of intelligent and righteous living or Zion.

A memorable libation I performed was for Earth Day, July 23, 2000, in Cincinnati, Ohio. Earth Day is the birthday of Ras Tafari, the King of Kings, the Lord of Lords, the Conquering Lion of the Tribe of Judah. I led the Rasta community in libation and poured water on the ground in four directions. This ritual reminded the community that to reach Zion and join the company of the blessed, one must strive to achieve bodily and spiritual purity. Another memorable libation was for Dayton's 2012 Juneteenth celebration. I called on the ancestors to teach the community "freedom is not free. We must make sacrifices to free ourselves." This libation was posted on YouTube.

In 2006, I poured libation at my Aunt Arona Moore Marshall's home going in Providence, Rhode Island. This funeral was the first time family asked me to perform the ritual. During the performance, my bracelet flew off as I sprinkled water to the four corners of the church. The dramatic moment was perhaps a protest that injustice and lies were present in the church.

Ten years later, I poured libation at the home going of my brother, Dechonte, in Brewerville. He died on his return from teaching in Asmara, Eritrea. I was the last person in the family to see him alive. I poured libation to ancestors who had gone before him. I focused on his musical journey and albums, especially *Liberian Libation*. His deeds and life were reflections of happiness, peace, beauty, and intelligence.

In libation for Aunt Lenora Zena Holcombe, who died at 95 years old, I read a poem I carried for the last two decades. I read it occasionally for inspiration. My libation to her paid tribute to her faith in God and love of life. I reminded our family and friends of her persistence and creativity. I spoke about her wisdom and love of beauty, nature, and family. I recalled her being a healer (nurse) who treated the sick and cared for the elderly.

I returned to Liberia to be with my mother during her transition to ancestry. Since then, I poured libations for the May 2019 home going of my Uncle Thomas Roberts and my mother Elizabeth Flowers-Gibson who died in Brewerville on November 29, 2019.

> "In the end, a man is alone with his fate."
> — African proverb

Boikai S. Twe

Chapter 21

Africa 2063

"An integrated, prosperous and peaceful Africa, driven by its own citizens and representing a dynamic force in the international arena."
— African Union Vision

In 2013, the African Union (AU) created the Seven Aspirations to celebrate its fiftieth year of existence. These aspirations were created through consultations with Africans in Africa and the diaspora. This bottom-up approach is different from past continental initiatives driven by so-called experts, leaders, and foreign aid. I chose to use these aspirations to describe a vision of Africa we hope to see by 2063:

1. A prosperous Africa based on inclusive growth and sustainable development

African psychology suggests that we live in a global environment of supremacy where White and Arab people are deified, and their lands are "holy places." Our people are seen as criminals and beggars who come from "shit holes." This darkness of enslavement and colonization forced African scholars to spotlight European and Arab control over our land and minds. This awareness led to the reemergence of African psychology which is grounded in science and truth-justice.

We will enjoy a higher standard of living and improved quality of life by increasing free trade among ourselves and demanding fair trade globally. Better jobs and incomes will come from defending ourselves and resources from foreign manipulation and exploitation. African states like Ethiopia, Rwanda, and Ghana have found ways to become more self-reliant and more Pan-African. The poverty and incompetence that dominate us in Africa and the diaspora will cease when we are educated about our rich cultural traditions and contributions to the modern world.

Ghana and Ethiopia have good educational systems that have improved economic development. The civilizations and states that we built along the great rivers of the Nile, Niger, and Congo suggest that we were the first humans to invent science, technology, arts, and government. Other firsts include religion, trade, navigation, medicine, engineering, and migration to spread these inventions. Enslavement and colonization robbed us of this memory and left us traumatized and in darkness.

We will question European and Arab definitions of reality and God. We will see, feel, and act in ways that affirm and protect our lives and future. When we recreate educational systems and reconstruct Pan-African institutions like AU and the Association of Black Psychologists, we will experience more prosperity and unity.

The present generation will be more confident that Africa's future is in good hands. This confidence will be based on a deep appreciation and study of Pan-Africanists like Marcus Garvey, W.E.B. Du Bois, Kwame Nkrumah, Julius Nyerere, Haile Selassie I and Rastafari. Narrow nationalism and tribalism will be overcome by economic and cultural cooperation.

We will become well-educated and skilled in science, technology, and innovation like South Africa, Egypt, and Ethiopia. We will make better use of local materials and modern technologies to build affordable homes and quality human services, sanitation, and healthcare. We can learn from Cuba's achievements in education and healthcare; developed despite fifty years of economic and cultural sanctions from the U.S.

We will modernize agriculture to increase productivity and food security. Too many of us are displaced and in refugee camps due to economic and political crisis. These crises will be reduced through sustainable and inclusive economic growth based on agriculture and resource management. Water security will need our attention due to climate change and thieves of natural resources. We will develop better control of marine resources and ports. The Atlantic and Indian Oceans have many opportunities for economic growth and natural resource management.

2. An integrated, politically united continent based on the ideals of Pan-Africanism and the vision of Africa's renaissance

After liberating ourselves from enslavement and feudalism in the 1950s and 1960s, Kwame Nkrumah envisioned a politically united Africa. Pan-Africanism challenges anti-Black racism in the diaspora and colonial domination in Africa. As an idea and movement, it assists in the establishment of a United Africa with world-class infrastructure and institutions. Our universities will offer degrees in Pan-Africanism, African Sciences and Arts. They will establish virtual universities dedicated to our cultural and political development.

We will have a single AU passport that will promote free movement across the continent and the diaspora. We will have a single air-transport network and an integrated high-speed train network. These transportation modes will allow us to travel from Cape Town to Cairo and Asmara to Dakar.

We will have regional common currencies and financial institutions that will promote African development and economic integration. We will have communication and regional connectivity to promote our renaissance and transnational development. African psychology will become a major area of study to better understand African/Black consciousness, heal disorientation and unleash potential. The unification of Africa will reduce displacement and mass migration. The corruption of leaders and civil servants will be reduced by increased checks and balances.

We will have more models of success to guide us as a result of economic cooperation and freedom of movement. A new Africa will emerge stretching across the globe. This development will elevate us from economic bondage and mental slavery to free human beings. African psychology will be a shield against Arab and European colonization and a spear against internal racism and colorism.

3. An Africa of good governance, democracy, respect for human rights, justice, and rule of law

Human development is normally a natural and orderly process involving the conditions of self, motion, order, form, and direction. Colonization and enslavement disrupted these natural conditions of development. As Africans, we will reclaim and better construct our identity, motivation, morality, systems, and goals. We will erect democratic institutions based on African models and the tradition of participatory development. We will create balance between urban and rural life and male-female relationships.

The abuse of women and children by traditions and systems will be eliminated. Truth, justice, and reconciliation will be restored in families, communities, and regions. Social security and protection of persons with disabilities will become priorities. We will strive to restore humanity and equity through development goals and constructions.

Our institutions will meet the basic needs of the poor and vulnerable. Revolutionary African leadership will be competent, more collective, and less self-serving. The use of organizations to secure human rights, justice, and good governance will be widespread in Africa and the diaspora. Institutional and anti-Black racism will be reduced through social interventions, rites of passage and local legislations. Media will play a greater role in the promotion of justice and rule of law.

African psychology will help to create more capable institutions and leadership based on our culture and science. A bottom-up approach to governance and policy making will strengthen human rights and empower the poor and neglected populations.

4. A peaceful and secure Africa

Africa has 80% of the United Nations peacekeeping missions. This statistic suggests that Africa has more armed conflicts and wars than any other place on the globe. The sale of arms in Africa is a lucrative business for Americans, Europeans, Russians, and Arabs. Our diversity is strength; however, it is being exploited by our enemies and arms merchants. We will reclaim our culture and consciousness to defend against self-destruction and imposed enslavement. We will maintain peace, security, and stability by creating the African Union Security Council which will coordinate and fund security and defense forces. We will not depend on the UN Security Council to fund our security.

We will develop and maintain a robust AU Defense and Security Force. The United Nations has been a tool of imperialism in Africa. Its predecessor, the League of Nations, was not a friend of Africa and its "peacekeeping" in the Democratic Republic of Congo led to Africa's longest civil war. African psychology will increase our memory to prevent manipulation and disorientation by religious and political criminals. The African Union's instruments on peace and security will be reformed and funded to "silence the guns" of civil wars. Our sovereignty will be defended by sacrifice and collective security.

We will restore truth, justice, and harmony to Somalia, South Sudan, Democratic Republic of Congo, Central African Republic, Libya, and Mali to prevent the capture of African youth and resources. Engagement in proxy wars to maintain foreign control of our resources and land will end. The U.S. is deploying troops and Special Operations forces in fifty of the fifty-five African nations. Many are on secret missions. We will not support missions against African people.

African psychology will develop interventions and rituals to deal with the trauma of war and abuse. African psychologists will play a crucial role in restoring self-confidence and skills as warriors, nation builders, and healers. African rituals and sacrifices will be performed to restore the well-being and humanity of the victims of war and crime. African science will be promoted and studied to prevent capture by materialism, capitalism, and religious fundamentalism.

5. An Africa with a strong cultural identity, common heritage, values, and ethics

Colonization and enslavement fragmented our identity, destroyed memories, and created divisions. African psychology will uncover our common heritage and commitment to what Marcus Garvey called, "One God, one aim, one destiny." Our sense of reality will not be defined by the United Nations, U.S., or EU. Our sense of history is being constructed to reclaim our ancestry of humanity. As the first humans, we cannot allow others to define us. Our contributions to the modern world will extend and transform our cultural identity. More Africans in the diaspora will return to Africa and embrace Pan-Africanism. These actions and investments will create businesses and institutions like the Museum of Black Civilizations in Dakar.

African psychology will increase scientific understanding of our identity which has been characterized as self-consciousness (state of being) and self-extension (state of becoming). We will be more conscious of our heritage no matter where we are in the world. African culture, arts and science will be better recognized and acknowledged for contributions to modern religions, arts, and sciences. We will expand Pan-Africanism in the global community. Rastafari will lead the march in the global expansion of Pan-Africanism and stay on the frontlines of the struggle for African cultural renaissance.

We will embrace our heritage as builders of civilizations and the bearers of truth and justice. We will build nations and rid ourselves of colonization and self-destruction.

African psychology will assist to realign ourselves to values of community, culture, and family. We will identify with people who are oppressed and will seek liberation and friendship. We will make May 25 Africa Day, a holiday of celebration and remembrance of the freedom fighters who made our liberation and unification achievable.

6. An Africa whose development is people-driven, relying on the potential offered by African people, especially its women and youth, and caring for children

Africa has the youngest and fastest growing population in the world. In 2050, one in every four humans will be African. This projection has led to youth seeking opportunities and revolutionary changes in their well-being. We began this march toward gender equality in all spheres as evidenced by Ellen Johnson-Sirleaf's 2005 election as the first African female president of Liberia. Seven years later, Nkosazana Dlamini-Zuma of South Africa became the first woman elected to head the African Union Commission.

The empowerment of African women can be seen in Rastafari, where Empress Menen, the wife of Emperor Haile Selassie I, emerged as the female principle of God. Women and girls will have greater roles in governance and access to educational, spiritual, and economic opportunities. Exploitation of women and girls will be exposed and uprooted to empower and heal the victims of abuse. Violence and discrimination against women and girls will be met with restorative justice from a new African leadership.

Children's rights will be enforced. Youth will be

empowered to contribute to local and regional development. African psychology in education will contribute to personal, familial, and community development. Self-confidence will be promoted in science, media, and the arts. Self-knowledge will be promoted to develop greater self-regulation and discipline. The history of African women in the liberation struggle and their leadership during times of crisis will be taught to build confidence and persistence.

Youth will be trained to be professionals, leaders, and active parents to the next generation. In 2030, 43% of all Africans are projected to join the ranks of the global middle and upper classes. Poor and working classes will be shown a clear path to economic self-determination. Libation will be poured in African ceremonies and celebrations to remember ancestors and connections to nature and the universe.

7. An Africa as a strong, united, resilient, and influential global player and partner

A united Africa will be a major partner in global affairs and will be able to better protect our interests at home and abroad. We will take full responsibility for financing our development. At this time, the African Union is largely financed by foreign aid. The Chinese built the African Union headquarters in Addis Ababa. We need to increase our economic and cultural exchanges with African communities. Moreover, African psychology will add value to our partnerships and markets by promoting fair trade practices in-and-out of Africa.

Africa will invest more in digital technology to accelerate development in the knowledge economy. Smart

Africa is a commitment by the African Union to make access to broadband and communication technologies affordable. It already gives Africans access to smartphones and mobile money. I use this technology in Monrovia to instruct U.S. psychology students online. My son, Emman, created Digital Good Times, a tech business that uses podcasts to promote digital technology and access in underserved communities.

Africa's role in global politics will match world powers like the U.S., Russia, China, and EU. We will have financial systems and public-sector revenues to complete vital infrastructure to better connect us. Our land will be better controlled and utilized for our benefit. Cooperative economics will be promoted for self-reliance, shared power, and shared wealth. The rights of minorities and oppressed groups will be protected and defended by the rule of law. We will once again be proud to be Africans and will not seek mass migration out of Africa. Our memory and confidence will be restored through Pan-African education and self-realization.

Chapter 22

Opening Zion's Gates

"I am not African because I was born in Africa, but because Africa was born in me"
—Kwame Nkrumah

The Promise Key is a pamphlet written and published by Leonard P. Howell in 1935 in Jamaica. His ideology became the key to the spiritual consciousness of the Rastafari community and the Pan-African movement in Jamaica. In this publication, Howell identified Emperor Haile Selassie I and Empress Menen Asfaw as "King Alpha and Queen Omega." In 1932, Howell began preaching and constructing a spiritual community based on the idea that Emperor Haile Selassie I was the Messiah of Black people. It was Howell who first identified the movement as "Rastafari".[32]

Howell opened Zion's gates with his writing and teaching during the decline of the Marcus Garvey movement, the British government's effort to suppress "revivalism" (religious cults) in Jamaica, and the invasion of Ethiopia by Italy in 1935. He inspired the African masses and established the first Rasta community at Pinnacle in 1940 in the hills of Jamaica. This 500-acre safe haven for Rastas

---

[32] Hill, Robert A. *Dread History: Leonard P. Howell and Millenarian Visions in the Early Rastafarian Religion.* Research Associates School Times and Miguel Lorne Publishers, Jamaica. 2001.

became one of the country's most economically productive and self-sufficient communities. It was officially wiped out by the colonial government in 1958. This community of some 3,000 Rastas, who were perceived as social outcasts and threats, brought the struggle for African liberation and Black Power to the world.

A second key to the gates of Zion is the chemistry and energy of blackness. Carol Barnes' book, *Melanin: The Chemical Key to Black Greatness*, suggests a unique link of "Black humans" to nature, environmental chemistry, and energy (See page 42). Francis Cress Welsing took a different perspective by looking at how lower levels of melanin in humans can explain White supremacy (See page 42). Disorientation and exploitation of Africans by Europeans and Arabs forced us to recognize that humans have sources of melanin which can be used to emancipate ourselves from mind control and economic bondage. Our natural environment and resources must be protected if we are to enter Zion.

My life-long experience with the Atlantic Ocean has been a major source of energy and inspiration for my mental and physical health. This natural source of melanin has opened the gates to truth-justice and well-being. It reminds me of where the bones of our enslaved ancestors are laid.

A third key to the gates of Zion is cultural, the Africanization of human culture. This unlocking of the gates has led to the construction of the African Union, the global expansion of African traditions and innovations, free and fair trade, and the increasing return of the African Diaspora to Africa. When I travelled to the U.S. to study psychology in 1973, I carried African music and literature with me. These cultural arts have influenced my spiritual, professional, and cultural practices. I have learned that everyone has value and deserves respect simply for being human.

We Are One
Africa is in our DNA
And in our hearts and minds.
It is not the place we are born
But dreams and spirit we possess.
It's the birthplace of humanity and civilization
It's the roots of our wealth, science, and art.

We've been robbed of memories and truth-justice
And must reclaim our economy, government, education
Science, literature, religion, and psychology.
We must reclaim Zion and our divinity
To bring us health and wealth.

Look for salvation in Africa
Not in Europe, America, or Asia.
No one can save us but ourselves.
Our ancestors will shield us
From the lies and destruction of captivity.
Let's become the divine light in our world of moral darkness.
—Boikai S. Twe

About the Author

Dr. Boikai Twe is best known for his passion for African literature and psychology. He is intentional about shining light on social justice, anti-Black racism, and the African diaspora. His goal: disband the lack of respect for Africans' contributions to the modern world and achieve global African unity.

Having spent most of his professional career as a mentor and college professor, he motivates youth to value self, develop character, and lead others. Dr. Twe was recognized as a Dayton Skyscraper, an artistic tribute to African American Heroes of Dayton and the Miami Valley Region. He received the Nia Award for his contributions to Sinclair College and the African American community.

This transcontinental author and educator presided over the Liberian Studies Association and organized conferences for Africanists in North America and Africa. Referred to as "Rasta," he has served alongside creative industry greats including Antonio "LA" Reid, BarbaraO, and Bing Davis.

On the heels of his first book, *Which Way Liberia: The Gun or the Book?*, Dr. Twe's sophomore book is a memoir of his tumultuous career in psychology, journey to enlightenment, and vision of African unity.

Dr. Twe holds a bachelor's in general psychology from Berea College, a master's in clinical psychology, and a doctorate in educational psychology from the University of Cincinnati.

For booking or more information, visit BoikaiTwe.com or drboikaitwe@gmail.com.

Boikai S. Twe

About Queen V Publishing

The Doorway to YOUR Destiny!

Go thou and publish abroad the kingdom of God.

—Luke 9:60 ESV

Committed to transforming manuscripts into polished works of art, **Queen V Publishing** is a company of standard and integrity. We offer an alternative that allows the message in YOU to do what it was sent to do for OTHERS.

QueenVPublishing.com

Serving professional speakers and experts to magnify and monetize their message by publishing quality books

www.ingramcontent.com/pod-product-compliance
Lightning Source LLC
Chambersburg PA
CBHW070602010526
44118CB00012B/1429